"*Treasured Places* is a love letter to America's towns and small cities, represented in its pages by a few dozen places that are special for their history, architecture, scenic beauty and—importantly—a strong sense of social cohesion and civic pride. Grab this little book, get behind the wheel, and set out on a cross-country tour of distinctive places. They're an antidote to suburban sprawl and impersonal metropolises, offering a pace of life that nourishes the soul.

"Interspersed among their delightful town profiles, authors Borut and McCaleb offer insightful short messages on the ingredients of healthy communities—something these experts on municipal governance know a lot about. Their personal list of *Treasured Places* probably includes a few of your own favorites, and it will introduce you to some unfamiliar gems you'll want to get to know."

—**Knight Kiplinger,** Editor in Chief,
The Kiplinger Letter and Kiplinger's Personal Finance

"*Treasured Places* takes us on a rewarding and insightful stroll across America. Borut and McCaleb share rich vignettes that capture the paradoxical blend that makes our nation so strong: individualism and love of neighbor. Our greatest hometowns celebrate their uniqueness and also strive to be welcoming. Our proudest community moments come when we are joined in common cause to lift up those who need us. This is a profoundly hopeful book, showing us that compassion, resilience, caring and love of home are the deepest roots in America.

—**Geoff Beckwith**, Executive Director & CEO
Massachusetts Municipal Association

"Having worked together with Don and Gary in the interest of our nation's cities, I am pleased that they have combined their years of experience to produce this collective celebration of America's cities and towns. This book should well serve as a reference for city leaders, who will find inspiration and motivation to preserve and protect their own local treasures. It also provides a useful checklist for those who might be seeking a way to personally travel through the storied pages of our nation's history as told through these *Treasured Places*."

—**Clarence Anthony**, CEO & Executive Director, National League of Cities, Washington, D.C.

"Gary McCaleb and Don Borut have undertaken a journey across our country's landscape into hometowns that foster the bonds of community and enrich the lives of their citizens. The result of their collaboration is a product revealing their shared belief in the vitality and energy of America's hometowns. In these pages you will find insight into the unique personality of each place, perhaps leading you to further explore those which intrigue you most. *Treasured Places* is a joy to read—hard to put down."

—**Lucy Allen,** Former Mayor
Louisburg, North Carolina

"Gary McCaleb and Don Borut have written an interesting and informative book that takes the reader on a journey that reveals the heart of these diverse communities. Their love of cities is evident and you can feel their emotion as they uncover each 'treasure.'"

—**Jim Hunt,** Former Mayor, Author, *The Amazing City*
Past President of National League of Cities

"The strength of America is evidenced by the diversity of its communities. Treasured Places highlights the beauty of nation through its true treasures, the cities in which we call home."

—**Lee R. Feldman,** City Manager, City of Fort Lauderdale, Florida

Don Borut & Gary McCaleb

CENTER for BUILDING
Community

TREASURED PLACES

Celebrating the Richness of America's Cities and Towns

Center for Building
Community

Copyright 2018 Donald Borut and Gary McCaleb

ISBN 978-0-692-12168-9

Printed in the United States of America

Cover design by Trey Jackson
Interior text design by Sandy Armstrong

Abilene Christian University
ACU Box 29136
Abilene, TX 79699

To
Carol Borut
and
Sylvia McCaleb

ACKNOWLEDGEMENTS

Lea Watkins has been an essential and invaluable part of the *Treasured Places* team from the very inception of the idea. Her insights, her attention to detail, her high standards, and her ever-pleasant personality have not only resulted in a higher quality manuscript but a more enjoyable process, and we are deeply grateful.

We also appreciate the design work of a talented young college graduate (class of 2017) named Trey Jackson for providing the cover for this book, and the thorough and detailed editing work of a good friend and consummate professional, Ron Hadfield.

And one final thank you to the "Front Line of First Impressions"—all the people we met during our visits to these Treasured Places—the waiters and waitresses in the restaurants, the hotel employees, the local shop owners and the long-time residents whose love and enthusiasm for their hometown provided an added quality of richness.

TREASURED PLACES

CELEBRATING THE RICHNESS OF
AMERICA'S CITIES AND TOWNS

CONTENTS

Macro-View: *Learning from Others* 111

Micro-Views: *Treasured Places of the Central United States* 115

Macro-View: *Creating a Sense of Place*......................161

Micro-Views: *Treasured Places of the West* 165

WHY I AM A PASSIONATE ADVOCATE FOR CITIES

DON BORUT

Place—where we live—is significant in defining who we are, how we see the world and what we believe is important. I grew up in New York City and consciously decided to attend a small college in the Midwest to explore beyond the comfortable bubble of the Northeast. This was not a rejection of my place, my home or my family: rather a desire to expand my view of America, if not the world.

Years later I came to appreciate the value, richness, diversity and excitement of "other" places. At the same time, when friends of my parents would argue that there is no city as special or good as New York, I was perplexed. They were both right as well as myopic. Being passionate about place is important. It is equally important to appreciate that your place doesn't have to be defined by devaluing or negating the unique qualities of other communities or cities.

As a child of the Kennedy generation, I believed I could make a contribution by working in the public sector, specifically in local government, first as the assistant city administrator in Ann Arbor, Michigan, and then as a staff member and deputy with the International City Management Association, and finally as the executive director of the National League of Cities. Working with the two national associations gave me the opportunity to not only visit and experience the remarkable diversity and unique values and qualities of cities and towns, but also to engage with elected and appointed officials who are passionate, committed and optimistic advocates for the places in which they live, work and represent.

My perspective on community and the importance of place is clearly informed by my experience and more particularly my engagement and appreciation of the commitment, engagement and leadership of those in appointed and elected positions in local government. As a prudent optimist, I see the cream in a half-filled glass of milk. At this moment in our history that optimism has been bent but not broken.

The current polarization in this country and the difficulty we collectively have in engaging with those with different perspectives, along with the demonization of those we don't know, is disheartening to me, the prudent optimist. The level of trust in elected officials is lower than it has ever been. That distrust is highest for those at the federal level, less so for those in state government and lowest for those leaders in local government. But the collective regard for local officials is still well below 40 percent.

Lost in this polarization, lack of public trust, and focus on that which is wrong or not working is the remarkable vitality of our cities, and what makes them unique and special. We too easily forget what is important about place, where we live, and why it is important to appreciate the richness of places outside of where we live.

In my position as the executive director of the National League of Cities, I saw my role as serving as the advocate for local government and those who served in leadership positions in U.S. cities, towns and villages. I gained enormous respect for those who made a commitment to serve and were prepared to make difficult decisions with the objective of improving their citizens' quality of life. Certainly, these men and women were not perfect. They have the same human needs, frailties and angst of all of us, but they were willing to act.

In speeches I made over the years I was fond of observing that running for public office at the local level is an irrational act. Individuals were scrutinized more than an amoeba under a microscope for below-market pay, to be confronted by citizens in the grocery store, restaurant or at a family outing . . . and for what, the right to make decisions that would tick off half their constituents. But they did it. They clearly needed strong egos, they struggled with the human challenge of doing what they believed was right and the reality of wanting to be reelected in order to continue to improve their communities. Most important, they cared, they believed in what was possible, and why their efforts were important to build the fabric of their community.

At the same time, these public officials have to balance their personal lives, spouses, children, and their own human needs. I remain impressed and in awe of local public officials for their almost universal ability to be passionate advocates for their communities, have a sustained sense of optimism and the ability to fend off the cynicism that today is endemic. They care deeply. It is through their perspective, engagement, and passion for their individual cities that I have been able to look for and appreciate each individual community regardless of size, location and population.

The cities, towns and villages these elected officials represent are a mosaic of our diverse communities, places that citizens can be proud of, if at times they take for granted, but more often than not, places that others can appreciate as tourists and visitors. This is not Pollyannaish, rather to respect that there is something special about place, every place, and it can be uplifting to experience the diversity of places that abound in our country.

The National League of Cities, through a network of state municipal leagues, represents more than 18,000 cities, towns and villages of all sizes. The vast majority of these communities have populations of less than 10,000. More often than not when the media reports on cities in the aggregate, they tend to focus on the very largest cities, often making generalizations about all cities from this perspective. Lost in this focus is the remarkable richness and unique diversity of communities, each with their own history, culture, geography, identity and sense of place.

Through my work, I was privileged to be able to personally visit cities, towns and villages in all of the 50 states, as well as work with and represent local elected officials all of whom were passionate advocates for what was special and important about the places they represented. More often than not it was through their eyes and the stories they shared with colleagues and members of Congress when they lobbied that I gained an appreciation of place and the rich pallet that is reflected in the thousands of American cities.

At the same time, much of my work and that of the elected and appointed local officials was to address the clear challenges their communities singularly and collectively were facing. This included infrastructure, housing, income disparities, race relations, as well as citizen antipathy to increased revenues for services they expected.

In addressing this broad range of challenges, there was always a restrained and unambiguous advocacy for what was unique, special and important about their communities. Whenever an NLC policy committee of local officials was deciding in which of their cities to hold a meeting, there were unrestrained presentations about what each could provide in terms of learning experiences for colleagues. And, indeed, my staff had the challenge of making sure those hosting a meeting didn't over-schedule the showcasing of the cities at the expense of time devoted to the meetings. In every single community there was something special, unique to place, that challenged the imagination of meeting attendees as well as providing examples that could be taken home and replicated.

During my NLC tenure, few if any elected officials served as a stronger advocate for what was special about their community and at the same time sought out and promoted what was special about other communities than Gary McCaleb. He and his wife, Sylvia, annually travel to cities, primarily small and medium size ones, to personally experience and identify the gems that give richness to place. He has been a Pied Piper promoting and encouraging not only local officials but also individual citizens and families to travel and visit well-known tourist destinations, as well as cities that are not generally in the guidebooks.

Therefore, I was especially pleased when Gary asked me to join him in putting together this book identifying and celebrating cities that have created an identity around something unique about their community, geography, history, culture or programs. The primary objective of this effort is to provide a treasury of places for families to visit and expand their appreciation of the richness of America's cities. It also is to provide examples of how cities, towns and villages have drawn on something unique and significant to enhance their economies, provide a focus for citizens to celebrate, and serve as a magnet for tourists.

To me it is important for all of us to have an appreciation, a sense of identity, and if not a passion, at least a positive feeling about our street, neighborhood and city as a way of affirming who we are. To be able to own what is special about place enriches all of us and provides a reason for community to prosper—socially, culturally, economically and humanely. This book is an attempt to give voice to a select group of cities that are wonderful, fun and educational places to visit.

CELEBRATING THE VARIETIES OF RICHNESS

GARY McCALEB

I suppose I have always had something of a fascination with cities and towns.

Perhaps it is because I have such good memories of the place where I spent the first 18 years of my life. Anson, Texas, was not a big city; the good memories of those years are captured in names, not numbers.

The rest of my life has been largely spent in Abilene, just 20 miles south of Anson. Over the years, Abilene, the place where, in the words of the song, "people there don't treat you mean," has been the place that my wife, Sylvia, and I have called home. It's the place where our daughter, Cara Lee, and son, Bryan, grew up.

And it's the place where I was fortunate to serve as mayor for nine years (1990-1999). It was during those years that my fascination with the places where people live was intensified. Opportunities to be involved with the Texas Municipal League, the National League of Cities, the U.S. Conference of Mayors and the International Union of Local Authorities provided perspective into cities, large and small, across America and throughout the world. Now, some 20 years later, I continue to enjoy and benefit from the relationships with former city officials, citizens who continue to care deeply about their communities.

In the year 2000, no longer an elected official but undiminished in my fascination with community, Sylvia and I began to spend some of our summer vacations on road trips across the U.S. We set a goal to visit "mid-size" cities in every state. As of this writing, our list of cities (using Charleston, ranked around 200th in population, as the largest city), has surpassed 300, in the 49 contiguous states.

Over the past 17 years, it has been an amazing journey. As friends have learned of our travels, several have asked for suggestions of places to include in their travels; others have encouraged a book.

As a result, Don Borut and I agreed to meet for a weekend in Williamsburg to discuss the possibility of doing a book together.

Over my nine years as mayor, I came to know Don as the executive director of the National League of Cities, but also as a true professional and a good friend. I am deeply grateful for his willingness to work on this project and I am confident this book would not have become a reality without his partnership.

From the outset, we agreed that we would not include any place in the book that at least one of us had not personally visited. In many cases, we both have first-hand knowledge.

Don and I feel the places included in this book are great representatives of the quality and variety of the American narrative as told in brief.

As I review the group as a whole, it is clear there is not one formula, they are certainly not all alike. In fact, there are many obvious differences. But a few common themes of each place seem to emerge from their stories:

- **History**: Early beginnings and stories continue to live in the American narrative of each place
- **Tenacity**: The life and vitality of the place have been preserved in spite of challenges and difficult times
- **Community**: Problems have been solved and victories have been won through togetherness and cooperation
- **Distinctivity**: The uniqueness of each place is valued and originality is preferred over sameness

And all has been done with a remarkable **Quality of Caring**. It's a caring that is authentic and unforced, a caring that comes from deep feelings about their town or city, and a realization that it has become a treasured place.

As you read the following stories, I hope you will listen for these themes to repeatedly surface as common characteristics, worthy of celebration and emulation.

There are many other cities and towns that have great stories to tell, and each in its own way is distinctive.

With nothing more than the mention of a city's name, an instant association and/or memory comes to mind. A few examples:

- Coeur d'Alene, Idaho—Beautifully located on the northern end of expansive Lake Coeur d'Alene, 25 miles in length with 109 miles of shoreline.

- Grand Forks, North Dakota—A true story of tenacity following the double blow of flooding and fire in April 1997. Eight of ten homes were damaged. This living story of courageous citizens committed to their community was captured in the words of a poster: "A Miracle in Progress. Grand Forks."
- Kearney, Nebraska—Its location, can't be missed when traveling on Interstate 80 because the Great Platte River Road Archway spans the highway three miles east of Kearney, marking the popular historic pathway of westward expansion by trails and rails.
- Lewiston, Idaho—Named in honor of Meriwether Lewis, and just across the Snake River from sister city Clarkston, Washington, is home to Lewis-Clark State College and the only seaport in Idaho.
- Kennett Square, Pennsylvania—Busy and picturesque tree-lined main street of the "Mushroom Capital of the World," claiming the production of a million pounds of mushrooms per day from area farms.
- North Platte, Nebraska—A town whose citizens permanently etched their place in history by voluntarily staffing the local railroad canteen to offer warmth and support to American soldiers en route to their World War II assignments. The visitor center at Union Pacific's Bailey Yards marks the location and Bob Greene tells the story in his book, *Once Upon a Town, the Miracle of the North Platte Canteen.*
- Burlington, Vermont—Located on the eastern shore of Lake Champlain, a four-block-long pedestrian outdoor mall, Church Street Marketplace was built in the early 1980s and continues to maintain a stirring energy and

vitality with over 80 shops and restaurants, giving reason for the American Planning Association to recognize it as one of America's "Great Public Spaces."

- Bennington, Vermont—A three-hour drive due south of Burlington, two stone monuments mark their place in history; the 300-foot-high Bennington Battle Monument commemorates the Battle of Bennington during the American Revolutionary War and the gravestone of four-time Pulitzer Prize winning poet Robert Frost lies in a quiet churchyard cemetery.

- Natchitoches, Louisiana—The downtown river walk on Front Street, including the preserved 100-years-old brick streets, draws thousands of annual visitors to this historic district which received the Great American Main Street distinction.

- Walla Walla, Washington—Tucked into the southeastern corner of the state and annually celebrating its agricultural heritage with the Sweet Onion Festival, Walla Walla celebrated a revitalized downtown not only through a tangible transformation but with an intangible quality of friendliness, which we personally witnessed and which has been repeatedly recognized in national publications.

And the list could go on . . .

But there is another list. The list of "Not Yet Visited." There are always more places we hear about—some on our list and highly recommended by others. They include:

- Lake Placid, New York—Holding the distinction of twice hosting the Winter Olympics.

- Hilo, Hawaii—known for its Rainbow Falls and Boiling Pots of bubbling basalt-lava rock pools.
- Vergennes, Vermont—the first city chartered in the state of Vermont (1788).

TREASURED PLACES
OF THE
NORTHEAST

ANNAPOLIS

MARYLAND

Settled in 1649 by Puritan exiles from Virginia, Annapolis not only experienced early leadership struggles, but also multiple name changes before it was incorporated in 1694. The city was named after Princess Anne of Denmark, later Queen of Great Britain. Little more than a village through the 17th century, it grew rapidly during most of the 18th century until the American Revolutionary War when it became a political and administrative capital, a port of entry and a major center of the Atlantic slave trade.

By 1780, Annapolis declined at the expense of Baltimore, as a port of entry, becoming dependent on oyster-packing, boatbuilding and sail making, reflecting its location on the Severn River with easy access to the Chesapeake Bay. Today the Severn and the many other tributaries make it a significant recreational sailing community. In 1845, the United States Naval Academy was located in Annapolis by then Secretary of the Navy George Bancroft, who was looking for a ". . . healthy and secluded location . . . in order to rescue midshipmen from the temptations and distractions that necessarily connect with a large and populous city."

The city also is the home of St. John's College, the third oldest school in the country, known for its curriculum based on the reading and discussion of "great books."

As a city, Annapolis has been a leader in recognizing the important contributions African Americans have made in Maryland and in the country.

Throughout history, African Americans have constituted a significant portion of Maryland's population and produced important national leaders in the long history from slavery to equal opportunity under the law.

Annapolis is a microcosm of the Maryland African-American heritage the city recognizes and celebrates in its Banneker-Douglass Museum and the African American Heritage Tour, a guided walking exploration which includes the Thurgood Marshall Memorial, honoring this heroic civil rights leader, the first African American member of the United States Supreme Court. There also is the Kunta Kinte-Alex Haley Memorial which celebrates the critically acclaimed book by Alex Haley, *Roots: the Saga of an American Family*, and the main character who arrived in Annapolis as a slave in 1767.

Other important Maryland African Americans celebrated and acknowledged in Annapolis include Harriet Tubman, often referred to as an American "Moses" for leading and helping hundreds of slaves escape into freedom and Fredrick Douglass, author, abolitionist, social reformer and first African American to hold a high U.S. position.

With a population of 35,000, Annapolis is the state capital, the home of nationally recognized educational institutions, the most celebrated recreational yachting community in the mid-Atlantic, and a city giving voice to the rich history, heritage and contributions of its African American community.

BAR HARBOR

MAINE

The area was first known as "Isles des Monts Desert" (Island of Barren Mountains), the name given by French explorer Samuel de Champlain in 1604.

The first settlement by Europeans in 1763 was given the name Eden, after English statesman Sir Richard Eden, who in the 1500s was one of the first to translate into English the early letters and accounts of European exploration of the New World.

The change of name to Bar Harbor occurred in 1918, apparently derived from the location of a prominent sand bar connected to the island. The last half of the 19th century was a defining era for Bar Harbor. As the impact of the Industrial Revolution grew, another movement became increasingly evident, perhaps best captured by a group of artists known as the Hudson River School of Painting.

Landscape artist Thomas Doughty's 1836 painting titled "Desert Rock Lighthouse" [Maine] was the beginning. It was soon followed by paintings by Thomas Cole with titles including "Frenchman's Bay" and "Mount Desert Island, Maine, 1845," as well as the work of Frederic Edwin Church which included "Fog Off Mount Desert, 1850" and "Lake Scene in Mount Desert, 1851."

During these years, Cole wrote, "Nature has spread for us a rich and delightful banquet. Shall we turn from it? We are still in Eden; the wall that shuts us out of the garden is our own ignorance and folly. . . . May we at times turn from the ordinary pursuits of life to the pure enjoyment of rural nature; which is in the soul like a fountain of cool waters to the way-worn traveler."

Henry David Thoreau's "The Maine Woods" was published in 1864, telling of his journeys through the backwoods with words such as "I am reminded by my journey how exceedingly new this country still is. . . . We walked over it with a certain awe, stopping from time to time to pick the blueberries."

As these artists—writers and painters—captured the beauty of the area, the visitors increased, some to enjoy a few days, others, with such names as Ford, Vanderbilt, Rockefeller, Astor and Carnegie, to build homes.

The motive of the artists and the new residents was two-fold—to enjoy the natural beauty and to protect it. A coordinated effort ensued to buy additional property, especially property that contained the wilderness beauty and scenes first captured by the artists. By 1914 more than 6,000 acres had been acquired with the idea of establishing a national park. In 1916 President Woodrow Wilson officially established the area as a national monument, which by 1929 had become Acadia National Park with Cadillac Mountain, the highest point, providing a beautiful view to this day. Acadia welcomes more than two million visitors each year, making it one of the most visited national parks in the United States.

John D. Rockefeller Jr. played a particularly significant role in the creation and expansiveness of Acadia National Park, donating about 10,000 acres of the land. He also funded a 45-mile-long carriage road system through the park and 16 stone bridges. In 2015, his grandson, David Rockefeller, celebrating his 100th birthday, provided an additional 1,000 acres to the Mount Desert Land & Garden Preserve.

Current citizens of Bar Harbor continue to honor the legacy of their predecessors. In 1947, a fire destroyed many of the Gilded Age mansions, but the town was reinvented and successfully restored by the resilient residents. Not only does Bar Harbor enjoy its national park, but in 2012 the American Planning Association named the town's Village Green one of the nation's top 10 public spaces.

A drive to the top of Cadillac Mountain is a good way to sense the serenity of surrounding Bar Harbor, and its storied history which shows "abundant evidence of benevolence and good will." It's as if you've arrived at the place of Church's painting, "Eagle Lake Viewed from Cadillac Mountain," and you reflect on his words, "We are still in Eden."

BERKELEY SPRINGS

WEST VIRGINIA

On the rainy night of March 18, 1748, George Washington rode into "ye fam'd warm springs," as recounted in his journal. He was a 16-year-old surveyor on his first big trip.

The maps, at the time, named the springs "Medicinal," and the number of visitors was growing as the stories of the springs spread.

Washington returned to "take the waters" numerous times over the succeeding years. He was apparently part of a group who decided to make these warm springs near the Potomac River the country's first spa.

Thus on December 6, 1776, the town of Bath was officially formed on 50 acres surrounding the springs. The name was taken from Bath, England, with lofty anticipation for its future.

Today, "the Country's First Spa" has two names. Bath is still the official name, but the "Post Office name" is Berkeley Springs. Regardless of the name, the warm springs still flow— 2,000 gallons per minute of 74-degree water.

For generations this natural asset has defined the identity of Berkeley Springs for its citizens and visitors from around the world. It has creatively promoted the unique and colorful history and developed additional assets that expand its vibrancy and attraction to visitors. Here is an example in which there is a collective commitment to historic preservation and a strategic openness for embracing other activities that enrich the quality of life for residents and guests.

Berkeley Springs is West Virginia's first certified arts town—and is consistently listed as one of the top arts towns in America. (It is estimated that more than 125 working artists live in Morgan County, population 16,000—Berkeley Springs, population 663, is the county seat.)

Visitors today stroll through history on a walking tour. Stops include Washington's Bathtub—a stone structure near the western edge of Berkeley Springs State Park, enclosing one of the five major springs Washington and his friends were believed to have used more than 250 years ago.

History and art have come together in this town with two names, and with its natural connection to water it makes sense that for more than 25 years Berkeley Springs has hosted the International Water Tasting and Competition.

CANTON

OHIO

Canton, Ohio, is to football as Cooperstown, New York, is to baseball. It is the home of the Pro Football Hall of Fame, the keeper of the holy grail of football history, heroes, and celebratory memorabilia: the city every football obsessed, passionate and slightly interested devotee must visit at least once.

In the early 1800s Canton was a small town lacking any transportation routes. Residents turned down an offer from the Ohio and Erie Canal planners to build a canal through the town, fearing disease from standing water. Again, when the town had an offer from the developers of the Cleveland and Pittsburgh Railroad to provide train service if the residents would pledge $10,000 for construction, the answer was "no."

Some 150 years later, however, the citizens of Canton took a very different position when it came to attracting the Pro Football Hall of Fame. In 1959 the local newspaper challenged the community with the headline PRO FOOTBALL NEEDS A HALL OF FAME AND LOGICAL SITE IS HERE. With the commitment of public land and money from a civic fund-raising campaign, this time Canton said "yes" to an opportunity to benefit the city.

In fact the first effort to create a professional football organization had its roots in Canton when the American Professional Football Association, the forerunner of the NFL, was founded at a Canton car dealership in 1920 with legendary Olympic gold medalist Jim Thorpe serving as its first president.

The deep historical connections to football were natural assets which were leveraged with initial and subsequent investment in the creation and expansion of the Pro Football Hall of Fame. It has extensive exhibits on the history of professional football, teams, inducted players, media exhibits, memorabilia, an extensive research and preservation facility, as well as ongoing events highlighted by the Annual Enshrinement Ceremony in August. The Pro Football Hall of Fame appeals to every level of fandom.

For those unimpressed or lacking passion for this national sport, Canton has additional historic attractions. It is the hometown of President William McKinley and the site of the McKinley National Memorial, and William McKinley Presidential Library and Museum. McKinley is famous for his front porch presidential campaign, speaking to more than 70,000 supporters and delegates who came to Canton to hear him.

The city also is home to the First Ladies National Historic Site, established in 2000 to commemorate all the U.S. First Ladies. In addition to the [Ida] Saxton McKinley House, the site houses an Education and Research Center and the National First Ladies' Library.

Here is a city that has found ways to celebrate its unique and diverse historic roots as the home of professional football and the home of President William McKinley to establish a community identity and attract thousands of visitors annually.

COOPERSTOWN

NEW YORK

Driving forward in space, you run backward in time, into a landscape of trees and fields, and, at the end of the road, a tiny town made up of picture-book houses set back on perfectly groomed lawns, gathered around a four-block-long Main Street interrupted by a single traffic light. This is Cooperstown, population 2,400, give or take the 400,000 visitors who come through every year to spend a few days amid a bit of demotic American history.—Jim Lewis, "Yes, There Really is a Cooperstown"

Arriving in Cooperstown is for many, entering a world com-posed of equal parts history, myth, memories and magic.

And it's been that way almost from the beginning. Its most famous citizen was James Fenimore Cooper, whose father founded the village in 1786. As the younger Cooper grew up, the surroundings provided rich inspiration for his writings, the best known being five historical novels, *The Leatherstocking Tales*, which include the "Deerslayer" and "*The Last of the Mohicans*." The main character, Natty Bumppo, is believed by some to be, at least loosely, based on Daniel Boone.

In 1851, Cooper died in his hometown at the age of 61 and is generally considered one of the most popular of the 19th-century American novelists.

If Cooperstown is not the Town That Invented Baseball, it is certainly the Town That Baseball Invented. . . . It's home to a number of other attractions as well, including two fine museums, an opera house, and an impressively appointed resort hotel, but the Hall of Fame is what makes it a destination.—Jim Lewis

The two museums are the Farmers' Museum, a well-designed experience into life and work in the 19th century, and the Fenimore Art Museum which includes art such as Thomas Cole's portrayals of America's wilderness and Gilbert Stuart's portraits.

"Glimmerglass Festival," a summer opera company, takes its name from Cooper's lake in his novels. Inspired by the landscape around him, Otsego Lake became "Glimmerglass" for the way the water became completely still and mirror-like. Today Glimmerglass is considered among the top opera festivals in America.

"Otsego" is the Iroquois word for "A Place of Meetings" and the Otsego Resort Hotel has lived up to its name since opening in 1909. Located on the lakefront of Cooper's "Glimmerglass," it maintains its place among America's best historic lakeside hotels.

. . . the Hall of Fame seems to me an unmitigated good. It's one of those rare places, like the Lincoln Memorial and the Hoover Dam, which are exactly what they're supposed to be. . . . —Jim Lewis, "Yes, There Really is a Cooperstown"

The Hall of Fame was actually the result of a rather incidental idea that continued to grow incrementally. According to John Thorn, the official historian for Major League Baseball, the story began in 1935 when Stephen Clark, vice president of the Otsego County Historical Society, paid $5 for "a homemade baseball, battered and beaten, the cover torn open . . . a baseball of great antiquity, hand sewn and of a small diameter like the few others that survive from the town-ball era . . . and displayed it in the historical society's exhibition room."

In 1936, the idea of a National Baseball Museum was formalized and other baseball memorabilia was slowly added, perhaps the most noteworthy was National League president Ford Frick's donation of the 1889 championship trophy of the New York Giants.

Frick also is credited with the idea of adding a Hall of Fame to the museum, and in 1937, the first Hall of Fame plaques honored five of baseball's best: Ty Cobb, Babe Ruth, Walter Johnson, Honus Wagner and Christy Mathewson.

Each year, baseball fans gather for an annual induction. Baseball commissioner Bowie Kuhn said the Hall of Fame induction is the "premier event of baseball's life. Cooperstown makes it so."

In July 1999, my son and I were among the crowds who celebrated the induction of Nolan Ryan, George Brett and Robin Yount. These are the days that many of the stars of past seasons make an annual migration. We stood on the porch of the Otesaga Hotel with Ted Williams, and at various places along the crowded streets we visited with Yogi Berra and Warren Spahn.

Where else, but Cooperstown?

Where else would a village of 2,000 have a baseball field that seats 10,000?

Cooperstown's most famous citizen, who may have never played baseball, wrote, perhaps prophetically, in *The Last of the Mohicans*, "History, like love, is so apt to surround her heroes with an atmosphere of imaginary brightness."

It's an atmosphere that illuminates Cooperstown, to the extent that its mayor describes it as "a magical place to live" from which you "may never want to go home."

In his book, *Why Time Begins on Opening Day,* Thomas Boswell observed:

> The modern world has aimed at Cooperstown and missed, much to Cooperstown's benefit and delight. The village, which has one traffic light, has been bypassed by every harbinger of progress from nineteenth-century canals and railroads to recent interstates; it has no industry but beauty, no operating principle but the preservation of an affluent civility.

DEARBORN

MICHIGAN

Dearborn, Michigan, is truly a remarkable city. It is where Henry Ford created the Ford Motor Company that played a transformative role in the history of America. It is a city that celebrates America's innovation and genius in all forms at the Henry Ford Museum of American Innovation. It is the home of Greenfield Village, the largest indoor-outdoor museum complex in the U.S. that provides experiences and presentations affirming important moments and changes in American history.

And it is a city that is a living, thriving community reflecting the fundamental strength of America by embracing and welcoming immigrants, reflected in the large number of citizens with Middle Eastern ancestry from Lebanon, Yemen, Iraq, Syria and Palestine.

Dearborn's recent history is in itself a reflection of the challenges and evolution of America. Henry Ford was a genius in creating the assembly line, paying employees what at the time was high wage, making it possible for them to purchase the cars they produced. At the same time he had strong anti-Semitic and racist views, but also was a leader in hiring African Americans and women. Yet the company and the city of

Dearborn were proactive in excluding African Americans from living in the city. Today, Dearborn is the antithesis of this past, one that is now open and welcoming.

Dearborn, like the arc of America's history, is a complex mix of the profound, the profane, the great, the good and the ugly. Its institutions and its vibrant culture acknowledges it all and as much as any city, brings the past alive and inspires through its museums that embrace American ideals. The Henry Ford Museum provides an opportunity to be immersed in the profound impact of transformational individuals such as Rosa Parks, who took a stand for equality as she sat on bus number 2857 in Montgomery, Alabama. Today, museum visitors may enter that same bus, carefully restored.

Where Henry Ford changed the landscape of America through the popular availability of the automobile, he supported the creation of Greenfield Village with historic structures celebrating earlier times and people, including the lab where Thomas Edison invented the light bulb, the Wright Brothers' workshop in which the earliest airplane was created and the buildings where Abraham Lincoln practiced law and Noah Webster compiled the first American dictionary.

Dearborn also is the home of the Arab American National Museum, the first in the world devoted to Arab American history and culture. "Through its interfaith council it regularly hosts gatherings where Buddhists, Muslims, Christians and Jews gather to celebrate the many masks of God."

Visitors are often drawn to Dearborn by the fame and reputation of Greenfield Village, only to discover the extensive Henry Ford Museum of American Innovation, the Arab American National Museum and inspiring cultural diversity that models the richness and strength of the United States.

GETTYSBURG

PENNSYLVANIA

Three days in July 1863 assured Gettysburg a lasting place in America's history, but the story of Gettysburg began more than 125 years earlier, in 1736, when the family of William Penn purchased the land known as Marsh Creek from the Iroquois Indians. Many of the first settlers were Scots-Irish who had fled Northern Ireland to escape persecution from England.

One of the early settlers was Samuel Gettys, who established a tavern in the Marsh Creek area. His son, James, laid out a town plan of some 200 lots including a central town square. As the population grew, the state legislature in 1800 designated Gettysburg the county seat of Adams County, named for the U.S. president at that time, John Adams.

By 1860, Gettysburg's population was approaching 2,500, and three years later General Robert E. Lee led his Confederate Army northward, meeting on July 1, 1863, the Union troops in a battle through the streets of Gettysburg. These three days are often described as "Civil War's bloodiest battle."

Then on November 19, 1863, President Abraham Lincoln delivered his memorable Gettysburg Address at the dedication ceremony of the Soldiers' National Cemetery.

To visit Gettysburg today is to visit a city-wide open-air museum. This is perhaps best illustrated at the Gettysburg Diorama, where it is possible to get a sense of the 6,000-acre battlefield, including a 30-minute sound and light show.

Tours of the battlefield sites can be accomplished by car or walking. A combination of both is probably best. There is much to see along the well-marked roads and paths, and even along the
downtown streets.

But there are also indoor places such as the Rupp House, where the John Rupp family of eight lived in the midst of the battle. Rupp wrote a letter a few days later in July, describing Union soldiers on his front porch and Confederate soldiers on his back porch firing at each other. Today the Rupp House reveals to visitors what life was like in Gettysburg during the Civil War.

And the Wills House was the home of Gettysburg attorney David Wills, where much of the work of arranging for the Soldiers' National Cemetery, including burials and the dedication ceremony, was coordinated. Two rooms have been restored to the 1863 times: Wills' office and the bedroom where Lincoln stayed the night before his famous 272-word address.

Among the many visitors to the Gettysburg battlefield was a young West Point cadet who in 1915 came with his class to study the battle. Three years later he returned as Capt. Dwight D. Eisenhower, with his wife, Mamie. He had been appointed commander of Camp Colt, the Army Tank Corps Training Center located on the fields of Pickett's Charge, to prepare World War I volunteers for overseas duty. Years later, in 1950, five-star Gen. Eisenhower returned to buy a retirement place. It became his retreat during his years as president. Sitting on the porch with world leaders provided an informal atmosphere with a view across an historic landscape, during which the conversation allowed him "to get the other man's equation." The National Park Service maintains the home and farm, which is open to visitors.

HOLLAND

MICHIGAN

In February 1847, a group of 60 men, women and children were headed to Wisconsin. They were leaving religious persecution and economic depression in the Netherlands, in search of a better place. The 47-day journey from Rotterdam to New York City had been wearisome, and winter weather caused further delays. As they reached an area in western Michigan, they chose to go no further. Hundreds of Dutch immigrants soon followed. This was the beginning of Holland, Michigan.

Eighty years later, in 1927, Lida Rogers, a biology teacher at Holland High School, made a talk titled "Civic Beauty," in which she suggested the city adopt the tulip and plant them in every yard. The idea was embraced and within a year, the community was importing 100,000 tulip bulbs from Holland.

The bulbs were made available to residents for one cent per bulb. The first advertisement, inviting visitors during Tulip Time in early May, resulted in 50,000 visitors. During the second year 175,000 came for Tulip Time.

Today, the visitors continue to come and enjoy the 4.5 million tulips that cover the city.

Tulip Time Festival has expanded to eight days, and includes daily performances of fully costumed Dutch dancers, concerts, parades and food.

When the results of the 2009 Gallup-Healthways Well-Being Index listing "America's happiest cities" were released, Holland (population 35,000) was among the very best.

So what's the explanation of this surprising result? An ABC News report touched on several factors, including:

1. **Churches**. If you ask the citizens of Holland why they're so happy, "religion is the first answer. . . . Known as the 'City of Churches,' Holland has 170 places of worship and even a college named Hope. The churches form an informal network that gets practical assistance to people who can use a helping hand."

2. **Culture of Giving**. Despite its 16 percent unemployment rate, Holland has more than 100 volunteer-based service organizations. . . . Holland along with a few other nearby towns in Western Michigan were recently named the second most generous region in the country by the *Chronicle of Philanthropy*.

3. **Community Spirit.** One citizen of Holland said, "My husband and I traveled a fair amount around the country and Holland has something that we very rarely find in other places. . . . It's a sense of community, a sense of acceptance—making people feel like they are special."

The ABC News report concluded: "Residents here know that solutions to problems are not found in the maze of ideas that come out of Washington, but from the rewards that come from caring about their neighbors."

"The Dutch, who founded this city 163 years ago, have a word for this—*gezellig*—which translates to 'close-knit community.'"

HOPE

NEW JERSEY

Driving across New Jersey, we decided to stop in the township of Hope. The Inn at Millrace Pond, a bed-and-breakfast, had been recommended as a good place for dinner and overnight—and we were not disappointed. In fact, as a bonus, we were treated to an unexpected journey back in time to the birth of our nation.

A plaque on the exterior of the stone structure introduced us to the historical nature of the place of our overnight lodging. It read:

> **Moravian Grist Mill**
> **Built 1769-1770**
> **Supplied Flour to**
> **Continental Army**
> **Under Gen. Washington**

Inside we discovered details of the story about the German Moravians who settled Hope in 1769 and established one of the earliest-planned communities in the country. Early planning maps reveal details of streets, homes, businesses, a school, tavern and church.

The primary reason for choosing the location was the availability of water power from Beaver Brook. The first industry was the imposing five-story Grist Mill and its Mill Race, which diverted a channel of water to the mill to run the grinding wheels, which produced the flour.

After 40 years of the "experiment" called Hope, the entire village was sold for $48,000 and the Moravians returned to Pennsylvania. The water-powered mill continued to grind the grain of local farmers for 136 years. The village of Hope was listed in the National Register of Historic Places in 1973.

And the story of Hope lives on.

Today, the township has a population of 2,000 and the Inn at Millrace Pond, with its exceptional dining room and 17 guest rooms for overnight visitors, proves once again the truth of author Joyce Carol Oates' observation:

> In America, history never dies—
> it's reborn as tourism.

LEWES

DELAWARE

The present location of Lewes, Delaware, was first colonized in 1631 by Dutch traders who named it Zwaanendael, meaning "Valley of the Swans."

So, on December 7, 1787, when Delaware became the first state to ratify the U.S. Constitution, the city of Lewes became the "First City in the First State" and continues to claim that place in history as part of its identify.

A walk along the streets of Lewes is an enjoyable and enlightening stroll through history.

The Zwaanendael Museum, distinctively designed to model the former City Hall in Hoorn, Netherlands, was built in 1931 to commemorate the 300th anniversary of Delaware's first settlement, and features exhibits that keep alive the stories of the early days for succeeding generations.

In the mid-1670s, England took claim of the area and the territory was conveyed to William Penn in 1682. The town was named Lewes (pronounced *Loo-iss*) in honor of Lewes, England.

In the heart of Lewes stands another local landmark, St. Peter's Church. Contained within its recorded history are the following lines:

St. Peter's Church has served the spiritual needs of this
community since 1680. Early settlers who were members
of the Church of England formed the first congregation.
Meeting in homes and later in the Court House, they
petitioned the Bishop of London to send clergy to serve
them and other churches in Sussex County. The first missionary arrived in 1708, but stayed for only a year. The
Sussex Mission owes its permanence to the Reverend
William Becket who came to Lewes in September 1721
and remained until his death in 1743. He is buried in St.
Peter's churchyard.

Other markers in the church graveyard, that extends to the
sidewalk's edge, tell of Delaware governors, tragic shipwrecks
and generous citizens.

Continuing the walk, near the waterfront is the Cannonball
House, now a maritime museum built in 1760. During the
War of 1812, the town endured a 72-hour bombing siege. To
this day, the impact of the bombs can be seen, including a
6-pound ball still embedded in the structure.

Over the years, the residents of Lewes have continued to
demonstrate their appreciation for keeping the story alive and
passing it along to the next generation.

In 1937, they decided to restore the names of the historic
streets of Lewes to their original colonial past, and today visitors can walk through history on streets named Pilottown Road,
Shipcarpenter Street, King's Highway and Knitting Street—further evidence that the townspeople enjoy, even take pride in,
living among the reminders of their rich history.

LEXINGTON, CONCORD, AND SUDBURY

MASSACHUSETTS

The first battle of the Revolutionary War was fought in Lexington and Concord in April 1775. On the evening of April 18, Paul Revere rode to Lexington to warn Samuel Adams, John Hancock and all the townspeople that the British were coming.

Today in Lexington, on the "Battle Green," the statue of the Lexington Minuteman stands as an historical landmark.

The Minute Man National Historical Park commemorates the opening battles "by protecting, preserving and interpreting the significant sites" such as the North Bridge and the Battle Road Trail.

And Concord is rich in literary history as well. Walden Pond, where Henry David Thoreau lived for two years in a shore-side cabin, provided inspiration for his most well-known work, *Life in the Woods*.

In the same area, one can visit the residence of Louisa May Alcott, author of more than 30 books, including *Little Women*, as well as the house of the American essayist Ralph Waldo

Emerson, who penned "Concord Hymn" which contained the words, "Here once the embattled farmers stood, and fired the shot heard 'round the world."

And only a few miles away in Sudbury is the Wayside Inn, said to be the country's oldest operating inn, beginning in 1716. But it was in October 1862, when Henry Wadsworth Longfellow visited the Inn, that a distinctive historical touch was added, as he made the Inn the setting for his book of poems, *Tales of a Wayside Inn*, which contained "The Landlord's Tale" with the popular lines:

> Listen my children and you shall hear
> Of the midnight ride of Paul Revere,
> On the eighteenth of April, in Seventy-five;
> Hardly a man is now alive
> Who remembers that famous day and year.

The Wayside Inn was renamed Longfellow's Wayside Inn around 1896.

The number of visitors to this mecca of American history continues to increase, reaching annual estimates of one million. Local historical society groups continue to refresh the experience from "worn-out to welcoming."

As a result, "the tourists are coming" . . . and they are staying longer.

MYSTIC

CONNECTICUT

The era of the whaling industry spanned the 19th century and probably experienced its best years in the 1840s.

And it was during those peak years, specifically 1841, that the whaling ship, the Charles W. Morgan, was built. Over the next 80 years the Charles W. Morgan made 37 voyages, ranging in length from nine months to five years. Surviving storms of all kinds, the whaling ship's work was done and at 100 years of age, was acquired by the Marine Historical Association (later to be known as Mystic Seaport).

Then, in 2014, after extensive repair and restoration, the Charles W. Morgan made its 38th voyage, a 16-week journey along the New England coast.

The story of the Morgan, the last wooden whaling ship in existence, is a tribute to the value of historic preservation. In 1971, a set of four commemorative stamps were issued. One of the four eight-cent stamps of historic landmarks features the vessel.

Today, this majestic maritime marvel sits proudly as an impressive centerpiece in Mystic Seaport, which includes a recreation of a 19th century seafaring village.

The village of Mystic, Connecticut, population 4,200, is the perfect home for the Morgan and for America's foremost maritime museum. Visitors are met with a life-preserver ring-shaped sign: "Welcome to Historic Mystic, settled 1664."

The name comes from the first settlers, the indigenous Pequot people, their term *missi-tuk*, describing a large river whose waters are driven into waves. The Pequot camped along the banks of the river which now runs through town.

Spanning the river is the Bascule Drawbridge, built in 1920, an appropriate landmark in the middle of Mystic. Children are entertained by continual crossing while waiting for the bridge to raise at 40 minutes past each hour.

The nautical theme is continued throughout the village. The Mystic Aquarium opened in 1973, and exhibits include sharks, an African penguin and the only beluga whale in New England.

In the shops, visitors can find maritime-inspired gifts such as handmade nautical knots for home decorating and special events, even a sailor knot bracelet.

Just across from the Bascule Bridge is the Whalers Inn, actually five buildings. The oldest is the 1865 House, once the home of a sea captain.

In addition to the year-round opportunity to spend a few days surrounded by maritime memories, Mystic Seaport also includes periodic special events. Two such examples are the Annual International Maritime Art Exhibition and Sale, featuring the best contemporary marine art, a favorite of the fall season, and the Chowder Days Festival, a time to enjoy the best of the New England specialty.

And when you've had your fill of chowder and seafood, there's always Mystic Pizza.

NEWPORT

RHODE ISLAND

The opening sentence in the "Brief History of Newport" produced by the Newport Historical Society states, "Since its founding by English settlers in 1639, Newport has bustled with diversity." Later in the article is this elaboration: "In the late 19th and 20th centuries various groups such as Irish, Greeks, Italians, Portuguese, Filipinos, Cambodians, and Hispanics joined groups such as Jews, African Americans and Native Americans who had been in Newport for some time, enriching the ethnic diversity of the town."

For more than 375 years, diversity, it seems, has been a continuing theme. Today, the story of Newport is a story of how diversity, not only in ethnicity, but in so many other ways, can enrich the sense of community.

Multiple chapters of the American narrative can be found nestled within the sites of Newport:

The Mumford House dates back to 1697 and is one of the oldest surviving houses in Rhode Island. It was damaged in 1766 during the riots of the Stamp Act. The Department of Interior included this house among the first designations of National Historic Landmarks. The house is located in the

Newport Historic District which covers 250 acres in the center of the city. Because of the expansive size of the area and the preservation of the colonial buildings, Steven Spielberg selected this district for the filming of the motion picture *Amistad*, which only enhanced the attraction to the area.

Trinity Church is another National Historic Landmark designation. This church, built entirely of wood in 1726, was based on designs of London churches of Sir Christopher Wren. The box pews remain, one of several distinctives that have been preserved through the years.

Touro Synagogue, dating to 1763, is another National Historic Site. The earliest known Jewish settlers were of Spanish and Portuguese origin. After the citizens of Rhode Island voted to ratify the federal Constitution, George Washington made a personal visit and following the visit, wrote letters to the citizen groups who had addressed him in Newport. His Letter to the Hebrew Congregation of Newport, on August 21, 1790, reassures those who had fled from religious tyranny to America that "every one shall sit in safety under his own vine and fig-tree, and there shall be none to make him afraid" and "the Government of the United States gives to bigotry no sanction, to persecution no assistance."

Each year, on or near the date of August 21, an assembly is scheduled in the Touro Synagogue for the reading of Washington's letter.

Mark Twain's 1873 novel, *The Gilded Age: A Tale of Today,* captured and gave a name to an era in which extravagance in homes became an obsession. Roughly approximating the time between the Civil War and World War I, many of the mansions, like the Vanderbilt home, The Breakers, have become museums. An estimated 400,000 visitors travel to Newport each year to this and other Renaissance palaces.

For more than 50 years (1930-1983) Newport served as the host site for the sailing "World Series," known as America's Cup. To many, Newport will always be first and foremost the "City by the Sea" and the "Sailing Capital of the World." Of the 3.5 million annual tourists to Newport, sailing is one of the big attractions.

The International Tennis Hall of Fame and Museum was established in 1954 and includes its own grass courts and the recognition of more than 200 inductees from 19 countries.

The National Museum of American Illustration opened in Newport in 2000, displaying "the most American of American art," including works by Norman Rockwell, N. C. Wyeth, J. C. Leyendecker, Howard Pyle and Maxfield Parrish.

Newport continues to add new chapters to its diversity of stories of ethnicity, religion, sports, art and architecture.

And added to it all is one other appealing feature: Walkability. Not only in the historic district, but on a 3.5-mile National Recreational Trail known as the Cliff Walk. On one side are the crashing waves of the ocean. On the other are the meticulously manicured green scapes of the Gilded Age mansions. It's Newport's memorable walk through history.

PETERBOROUGH

NEW HAMPSHIRE

In one of the earliest existing documents regarding Peterborough, the first settlers wrote in the mid-1700s that they had "cultivated a rough part of the wilderness into a fruitful field" and the primary needs for incorporation included a meeting-house, road repair and the building of bridges.

Much of Peterborough's identity can still be found within those lines. While parts of the wilderness have been very productively cultivated, the preservation of wilderness beauty is an asset as well. And the roads and bridges provide for a continuing flow of visitors to the extent that tourism is a major economic component—a "wilderness tourism" comprised of such things as hiking trails, cross country skiing, kayaking, wildflower photography, cycling, fishing and bird watching—and one more thing: inspiration.

In 1896, composer Edward MacDowell and his pianist wife, Marian, bought a farm in Peterborough where "they spent summers working in peaceful surroundings." It was in that setting that Edward, one of America's first great composers, said he "produced more and better music." Unfortunately, Edward became ill and prematurely died. But he had discussed with Marian how he wished other artists could have the same creative experience which he had enjoyed. This idea became known nationwide as the "Peterborough Idea" and in 1906 Grover Cleveland, Andrew Carnegie and J. Pierpont Morgan, among others, established a fund in Edward's honor and the MacDowell Colony became a reality.

In 1997, the National Medal of Arts was awarded to The MacDowell Colony for "nurturing and inspiring many of this century's finest artists."

By 2016, more than 7,000 artists had received Fellowships to the Colony, with 250 or more arriving each year. Among these composers, playwrights, poets, artists and writers are winners of at least 77 Pulitzer Prizes.

While at MacDowell, Willa Cather wrote *Death Comes to the Archbishop*, Aaron Copland composed *Billy the Kid*, James Baldwin wrote *Giovanni's Room*, Leonard Bernstein composed his *Mass,* and E.L. Doctorow wrote *Billy Bathgate*.

And Thornton Wilder wrote *Our Town*—the 1938 recipient of the Pulitzer Prize for Drama. A perennial favorite, it won the Tony Award for Best Broadway Revival 50 years later.

Brooks Atkinson's review of the play included the following: "Taking as his material three periods in the history of a placid New Hampshire town, Mr. Wilder has transmuted the simple events of human life into universal reverie."

Today, this drama of life in the small village of Grover's Corners in the early 1900s has become an American classic and Wilder reportedly considered it his favorite of all his works.

No one seems certain of the extent to which the fictional Grover's Corners is based on Peterborough—but most agree there was at least some influence—sufficient enough that Peterborough is unofficially, at least, referred to as "Our Town."

There is, additionally, the possibility that the name Grover's Corners was a derivation from Grove Street, which intersects with Main Street in Peterborough.

The relationship between the Colony and Peterborough is celebrated with regularity. MacDowell Downtown occurs on the first Friday, from March to November, when MacDowell artists share their music, film, readings and performances with the public.

In *Our Town,* when Mr. Webb, a local citizen, is asked if there is any "love of beauty in Grover's Corners," his reply, in part, is ". . . maybe this is the place to tell you that we've got a lot of pleasures of a kind here: we like the sun comin' up over the mountain in the morning, and we all notice a good deal about the birds. . . . And we watch the change of the seasons. . . ."

> There is a certain natural beauty captured in the plurality
> of the possessiveness of the title—*Our Town*.

STOCKBRIDGE

MASSACHUSETTS

The village of Stockbridge provides an unusual opportunity: a visit to three historic houses which spans over 250 years and the story from each house is based in three different centuries.

The first story begins around 1740 when a young missionary named John Sergeant built a house for himself and his new wife. Until this time, Sergeant had been living in a cabin for about five years, after the Mohicans had given him permission to live among them. The house Sergeant built still stands, although it has been carefully moved to a different location. It is called the Mission House, and contains a collection of 18th-century furniture, providing an insight into colonial history and the Native Americans who first lived in western Massachusetts. Sergeant was succeeded by Jonathan Edwards, who was part of the First Great Awakening, a Protestant movement in the American colonies. The Mission House is listed on the National Register of Historic Places and named a National Historic Landmark.

The second story is found in Chesterwood, a National Trust Historic Site, and the summer home and studio of Daniel

Chester French, known as America's foremost public sculptor. His 1874 sculpture, *Minute Man*, at the Old North Bridge in Concord, Massachusetts, was an early factor in establishing his reputation and likely a key to his selection to create the Abraham Lincoln statue for the Lincoln Memorial in Washington, D.C. Three plaster models of the Lincoln statue, along with sketches and other works by French, are a part of the collection at Chesterwood. French was selected by the Lincoln Memorial Committee in 1914. The seated Lincoln figure is 19 feet in height and was unveiled in May 1922, a project spanning more than seven years.

The third story is contained in the collection of the Norman Rockwell Museum, the "Home for American Illustration," and Stockbridge was home for Rockwell for 25 years, until his death in 1978 at the age of 84. Rockwell was fond of his hometown, saying it captured "the best of America." Over the years, it seemed that most of the people who lived there had been a subject in one of his famous paintings. He once remarked, "Without thinking too much about it in specific terms, I was showing the America I knew and observed to others who might not have noticed."

In 1916, at the age of 22, Rockwell's first cover of *Saturday Evening Post* was published. Over the next 47 years, he would produce another 321 covers. Rockwell considered the cover of the *Saturday Evening Post* as "the greatest show window in America." For so eloquently telling the story of America in his paintings, Rockwell received the Presidential Medal of Freedom in 1977.

Perhaps one of the lasting Norman Rockwell favorites became known as "Home for Christmas"—a pullout illustration originally done for *McCall's* magazine in 1967. The project reportedly began in 1956 and took 11 years to complete. It became a perennial image of everyone's ideal Christmas scene, but it was especially meaningful to the citizens of Stockbridge.

The painting of Main Street at Christmas fostered an annual Stockbridge Christmas tradition during which the painting is re-created. For more than 20 years everything along Main Street, even the vintage cars, has been positioned just as it was in the painting. The original now hangs in the Norman Rockwell Museum.

Chief museum curator Stephanie Plunkett said the painting "was meant to evoke the quintessential American holiday, to evoke a sense of warmth and peace . . . that would make people all over the country, possibly all over the world, feel as though they had come home for Christmas."

COMMUNITY RECOGNITION

DON BORUT

When I was assistant city administrator in Ann Arbor, Michigan, early in my career, I was tasked with working with a citizens group to develop an application for the National Civic League's All- America City award. Why we would spend the time to compete for an award that involved identifying some activity or program that we had undertaken seemed to me at this naive stage of my life a waste of time. How wrong I was!

The process involved working with community groups to identify a successful community program, preparing a written proposal and presenting it to a panel of judges. Only after Ann Arbor was chosen as an All-America City did I fully understand the significance, a significance well beyond the specific program for which the city was recognized. For the citizens, the program morphed into Ann Arbor being recognized as one of the best cities in America. City Hall could not print up enough All-America decals requested by citizens to put on their bumpers, front windows and bicycles. This was a national affirmation of their home, their place, a confirmation that where they lived was indeed special and important, something they believed. This is not to say that everyone exhibited or expressed these feelings, but it was so broad a reaction that I was compelled to understand the importance of place and personal identity.

Many years later I served on the judging panel for the All-America City awards and gained an even greater appreciation of the significance of this recognition and the process. In addition to providing written applications, cities made formal presentations to the judging panel. More often than not communities sent delegations of citizens to represent and present their program to the judges. It was not the slick PR presentations that won the day: rather it was the personal stories told by citizens, often nervous but always passionate about efforts that demonstrated collaboration, engagement and some level of change or improvement in their community. Often it wasn't the most dramatic initiative, but one in that particular community that was dramatic in terms of the obstacles they overcame.

The city of Jackson, Michigan, more than any community that came before the judging panel on which I served, personifies this fundamental point. This was a city in the midst of an unprecedented economic downturn, even a depression, as a result of the closing of manufacturing auto parts plants. However, even at this moment deserving of community angst, citizens and community groups found creative ways to address economic challenges and remain enthusiastic advocates, committed to their place, the city of Jackson.

Place clearly matters and citizens to a great degree want to feel there is value and something special about the community in which they live. An outside observer might wonder what is so special or why residents seem to be such partisan advocates for place, but they would be missing the human need for community identity and at some level, commitment to home, whether it's their street, neighborhood, city, region, state or nation.

The stories we have presented in this book are rich examples of communities in which there is not only something unique that enriches the lives of citizens in these places which they promote, but also communities that have used their special something to enhance the economy and quality of life for the citizens, and to provide an opportunity for visitors to experience what is truly special and unique.

TREASURED PLACES

OF THE

SOUTH

ASHEVILLE

NORTH CAROLINA

The 90,000 citizens and the 9 million annual visitors seem to agree that Asheville is a treasured place. The reasons are varied but often coalesce around the theme of preservation, whether applied to the walkable downtown, the storied history or the scenic beauty of the Blue Ridge Mountains.

In fact, there is a Walking Tour Guide available to any visitor who walks "in Thomas Wolfe's shoes" through the Asheville "that he saw in his lifetime" and "that he wrote about in his books."

Among the many possible stops along the tour is one of American literature's most famous landmarks, a rambling old Victorian boarding house that was the setting of Thomas Wolfe's autobiographical novel, *Look Homeward, Angel.*

During his boyhood years, Wolfe lived in the house which is now designated a National Historic Landmark and a museum. The house, built in 1883, was originally named "Old Kentucky Home"; in his book, Wolfe named it "Dixieland." Today it is the "Thomas Wolfe House."

Look Homeward, Angel was published in 1929 and has never been out of print since. The story was adapted as a

Broadway play in 1957 and won a Pulitzer Prize and several Tony nominations.

The book's title seems related to several stone angels which Wolfe's father sold in his tombstone shop. One of those stone angels is located in the Oakdale Cemetery in Hendersonville, about 20 miles south of Asheville. It has been observed that the angel is facing east, as if looking back to the beginning.

The year 1895 marked the opening of what has been called "America's Castle," more specifically the Biltmore. Recently it has been considered America's version of Downton Abbey. George Vanderbilt, the grandson of industrialist Cornelius Vanderbilt, had visited the Blue Ridge Mountains and was convinced they provided the ideal setting for a country home. The result was a 250-room French Renaissance chateau, designed by architect Richard Morris Hunt. The gardens and grounds were designed by landscape architect Frederick Law Olmsted. Vanderbilt had engaged two of the foremost designers of the 19th century.

When the American Institute of Architects celebrated its 150th anniversary in 2007, a survey was sponsored to determine America's Favorite Architecture, which resulted in a list of the top 150. The top 10 included six from Washington, D.C., and two from New York City. The other two were San Francisco's Golden Gate Bridge and the Biltmore Estate of Asheville.

And the Biltmore has played other roles in American history. In 1942, during the war, the National Gallery of Art moved priceless pieces of its collection to the safety of the Biltmore.

In 1956, the Biltmore was first used as the setting for a motion picture. *The Swan*, starring Grace Kelly, was her last film.

Other movies have used the Biltmore Estate and the beautiful surroundings in and around Asheville as a setting. *The Last of the Mohicans* was shot exclusively in the mountains around Asheville and the film based on the book *Cold Mountain* is about the area around the real Cold Mountain. The author, Charles Frazier, received the 1999 U.S. National Book Award for Fiction and today many hikers walk the sometimes difficult but always stunning Cold Mountain trails just outside Asheville.

From the heights of the Blue Ridge Mountains, with a view of Asheville, the traveler's thoughts might intersect with words from Wolfe's *Look Homeward, Angel:*

Yet, as he stood for the last time
by the Angels,
he was like a man
who stands upon a hill
above the town he has left.

But before leaving, spend some time on the Urban Trail. It's Asheville's way of combining walkability and history into an outdoor museum. Among the special features is one of the largest and best groups of Art Deco buildings in America. The First Baptist Church (1925-26) is one of the most notable examples. With the help of the self-guided tour map, we had the choice of following the 1.7-mile trail with 30 stations (each includes a bronze commemorative plaque or art piece as an elaboration on the storied past); however, we soon chose the flexibility of mixing the historic stops with contemporary shops—combining the past with the present Asheville, in a thoughtful and well-designed museum-without-walls experience.

ATHENS

GEORGIA

A mong the many population centers in America, it might be difficult to find a place that could make a stronger case for being a true college town than Athens, Georgia.

The University of Georgia was incorporated by an Act of the General Assembly on January 27, 1785, thus becoming the first state-chartered university in the U.S. And when the University of Georgia opened for classes in September 1801, it preceded the official beginning of the city. The city was named Athens—to honor the great city of the golden age of Greece—and was incorporated some five years later, December 8, 1806. The first class of 10 students graduated in May 1804. The first permanent brick building on the campus was completed in 1806 and still stands today.

The city of Athens is self-described as "Just below the foothills of the Blue Ridge Mountains, near the confluence of the North and Middle Oconee Rivers. . . . Among the rolling red clay hills of North Georgia, a city and a university grew into a center of culture."

And if there is a second theme that joins together with "education" it would seem to be "preservation."

The National Historic Register includes 16 historic dis-
tricts and 35 other sites within Athens. The Athens Welcome
Center is appropriately located in the Church-Waddel-Brumby
House, which dates to the 1820s and includes a museum and
authentic period décor. It is believed to be the oldest surviving
residence in Athens.

The Welcome Center also is the first of 48 stops on the
Athens Downtown Walking Tour, a self-guided walk with a
map and a brief paragraph about the history and significance
of each. Included in the list is number 28, The Arch, one of the
popular photo opportunities in Athens, which symbolizes the
main entrance, or the gate from the city onto the campus.

Stop number 45 is another high priority symbol that
brings ancient and contemporary history together. The statue
of Athena was an effort of local citizens to commemorate the
1996 Olympic games and the city's name with the original
Greek Olympic games. In fact, even though Atlanta was the
host city, many Olympic events were held in venues around
Atlanta. Athens hosted the women's soccer final game in
Sanford Stadium on the campus of the University of Georgia.
And it was there that the U.S. defeated China 2-1 for the
gold medal.

The 9-foot-tall statue of Athena, Greek goddess of wisdom,
faces downtown, the heart of the city. On the base beneath
Athena, the words of the Athenian Oath are inscribed. Words
from the golden age of Greece, pledged by the youth when
they reached the age of 17. Words that are just as appropriate
in Athens, Georgia, and all our cities:

> We will never bring disgrace on this our City
> by an act of dishonesty or cowardice.

We will fight for the ideals and
Sacred Things of the City both alone
and with many.
We will revere and obey the City's laws
and will do our best to incite a like
reverence and respect in those above us
who are prone to annul them or set
them at naught.
We will strive increasingly to quicken
the public's sense of civic duty.
Thus in all these ways we will
transmit this City, not only not less,
but greater and more beautiful than
it was transmitted to us.

BEAUFORT

SOUTH CAROLINA

Anyone searching for information about Beaufort, South Carolina, will likely run across these two statements: "a rich history spanning over 500 years" and "currently considered by many as the best small Southern town in America."

And it's the way the people of Beaufort so skillfully, even artfully, blend past history and contemporary life that continues to draw thousands of visitors.

The natural starting place seems to be Waterfront Park, the connecting point of the waters which brought early explorers and the land which welcomed new settlers.

Two rather well-established festivals reach back into those early years.

The Original Gullah Festival draws more than 30,000 people to the Waterfront Park area for three days each May. The Gullah heritage, as descendants of slaves, celebrates the art, authentic cuisine and cultural influence on the Beaufort islands area. The festival promotes itself as "an example for others to witness of a community coming together in unity to celebrate our shared unique rich history."

The Penn Center Heritage Days is a November celebration of one of the first schools for formerly enslaved Africans. The Penn School was founded in 1862 and has welcomed more than 40,000 annual visitors to its Beaufort County campus.

Two other festivals celebrate more recent history. During the 1980s and '90s, Beaufort became a popular location for filmmakers, including the 1995 Academy Award-winning *Forrest Gump*. In 2007, the Beaufort International Film Festival was begun with 500 in attendance. In its 10th year, 12,000 people from 37 states and five countries attended the five-day festival, ranked in the top 25 film festivals in the world.

The author Pat Conroy, a Beaufort resident, saw two of his books, *The Great Santini* and *The Prince of Tides,* made into movies in his hometown, and following his death, the first Pat Conroy Literary Festival was held in October 2016.

There are other festivals, but even when there is no festival, there are more than 25 grand Antebellum houses, dating back to the 1750s, within walking distance of Waterfront Park. And the Lady's Island Garden Club has designed a 1.4-mile self-guided Tree Walk, a creative combination of Spanish moss-covered trees and historic homes in a walkable 30-point map.

Upon leaving Beaufort, about 15 miles along the way to Interstate 95, there's one more important stop—a reminder that all the days in this historic Low Country have not been days of celebration. The Old Sheldon Church Ruins, with parts of its large classic brick columns and arches still standing, are found in a hushed opening among spreading tree branches. A stone tablet was attached to some of the partly blackened bricks in 1937. The words include the following:

Built Between 1745—1755
Burned by the British Army 1779
Rebuilt 1826
Burned by the Federal Army 1865

The ruins are on private property. Information provided by the owner contains this sentence: "From its first service in 1757 to its present peaceful setting, the church has followed the travails of our nation's history."

The past is indeed prologue, in so many ways, to the Beaufort of the 21st century, and the reason for much of its continued vitality.

As we walked among the vibrant downtown shops spread along Bay and Carteret Streets, just behind Waterfront Park, I asked one of the many local proprietors how she had kept her shop open for more than 20 years.

"Downtown is successful," she said, "because we've lived here and we care about this place and we work hard to take care of it. We are proud of Beaufort and we like to brag about our town."

In the prologue for *The Prince of Tides*, Conroy expressed a similar pride:

> To describe our growing up in the low country of South Carolina, I would have to take you to the marsh on a spring day, flush the great blue heron from its silent occupation, scatter marsh hens as we sink to our knees in mud, open you an oyster with a pocketknife and feed it to you from the shell and say, "There. That taste. That's the taste of my childhood." I would say, "Breathe deeply," and you would breathe and remember that smell for the rest of your life. . . . I am a patriot of a singular geography on the planet.

CHARLESTON

SOUTH CAROLINA

Lists are endlessly made of America's top cities—top cities for tourists, top cities for history, top cities for culture, and on and on.

One that seems to find its way into many of the "top cities" lists is Charleston. Perhaps that's the reason for *Forbes Life's* recent and singular compliment: "Pound for Pound, America's Finest City."

One of the continuing challenges facing a city is to resolve the tension between its past, present and future. That's a challenge Charleston has met well.

As Richard Nalley writes, "The place, to put it mildly, is not afflicted with the amnesia effects of American Progress. Around here, the new must always accommodate itself to the stubborn tenacity of what came before."

The Civil War started at Fort Sumter in Charleston's harbor, a city that played a major role in enslaving Africans coming to America. It has long acknowledged this history and at this writing its longtime mayor Joseph P. Riley Jr. is raising funds to build a world-class museum "to highlight the experiences and contributions of Africans brought to America against their will." It is where the novel and opera *Porgy and Bess* is set.

The 2000 census listed Charleston's population as 96,650—proving a rank with the best is in reach even when ranking with the biggest isn't.

I'm reminded of the words of Mayor Riley who said several years ago, "Sometimes, if you paint on a smaller canvas, you can make a more beautiful picture."

The Charleston canvas is imbued with the colors and elements of a city continuing to enhance the quality of life for its citizens and all who are drawn to it. It is reflected in the commitment to serve and uplift everyone, the commitment to the built environment and the rich mix of cultural and artistic programs and activities.

As the creator of the Mayor's Institute on Urban Design, Riley's leadership in Charleston has served as a textbook model for mayors across the country in appreciating the significance of design, preservation and the built environment as critical components enhancing the quality of life for citizens and serving as a magnet for visitors from around the world.

When Pulitzer Prize-winning Italian composer Gian Carlo Menotti sought the American counterpart to the Festival dei Due Mondi (Festival of Two Worlds) in Spoleto, Italy, "he searched for an American city that would offer the charm of Spoleto, Italy, and also its wealth of theaters, churches, and other performance spaces. Charleston, South Carolina, was the perfect counterpart. A city that had been home to the first theater and the first ballet company in America, and is still home to the oldest musical organization in the country, Charleston is small enough to be dominated by non-stop arts events during the 17-day festival, but also large and sophisticated enough to provide a knowledgeable audience and appropriate theaters."

By identifying and building on the unique history, location and built environment, and enjoying the leadership of a mayor with a clear vision and the ability to embrace the creative ideas of others, Charleston has truly created a beautiful picture on a smaller canvas.

CHARLOTTESVILLE

VIRGINIA

Charlottesville was named in honor of Princess Charlotte, who became Queen of England when she married King George III in 1761. However, the prevailing aura surrounding this city is not connected to the former Queen of England but to the life and work of the third president of the U.S., Thomas Jefferson.

And Charlottesville's place in American history was further assured when it also became the home of the nation's fourth and fifth presidents, James Madison and James Monroe.

Jefferson, at age 26, began to design and build his Monticello (derived from Italian for "little mount"), which is the familiar imprint on the U.S. five-cent coin. Monticello is the only house in America on the World Heritage List.

When Jefferson stepped away from what he called the "splendid misery" of the presidency in 1809, he returned to his Monticello. A walk through the premises clearly illustrates how he spent his last 17 years: writing letters, inspecting his plantation, conversing with many visitors and reading books. "All my wishes," he said, "end, where I hope my days will end, at Monticello."

He died on the 50th anniversary of the Declaration of Independence, July 4, 1826, at the age of 83. John Adams, whom Jefferson had succeeded as president, died on the same day.

Jefferson was buried at Monticello. On the gravestone visitors may read the words which Jefferson had chosen: "Here was buried Thomas Jefferson, Author of the Declaration of Independence, of the Statute of Virginia for Religious Freedom, and Father of the University of Virginia."

The last words of his self-written epitaph reveal his feelings for the place that has been called the "Most Beautiful Campus in America," "America's Public University" and "Jefferson's Masterpiece." Jefferson called it his "Academical Village." In 1987 UNESCO designated Monticello and the University of Virginia as World Heritage Sites.

The campus was designed around two distinctives: The Lawn and the Rotunda. Both were used to create an environment for students and faculty to live, interact and learn from one another. Two of the favorite traditions are Jefferson's Birthday and the Lighting of the Lawn at Christmas.

The early name for the road running east and west across Virginia was Three Notch'd Road, a name apparently inherited from three notches cut in trees to keep the travelers from losing their way. It eventually became the well-traveled connector between Richmond, the home of the state capital, and Charlottesville, the home of Jefferson and, not far away, his younger friend and presidential successor, James Madison.

Madison had a primary role in the development of the Constitution and Bill of Rights and earned Jefferson's great appreciation by affirming the human rights to religious liberty, freedom of speech and due process.

Following their years in the White House, James and Dolley Madison retired to Montpelier and to two of his favorite things: farming and his papers.

A visit to this home of one of America's founding fathers is self-described as an opportunity to engage "with the enduring legacy of Madison's most powerful idea: government by the people."

A third president and frequent traveler on Three Notch'd Road (now closely patterned by U.S. Interstate 64) was James Monroe, a governor of Virginia and leading negotiator of the Louisiana Purchase.

The Monroe home, called Highland, is sometimes referred to as a cabin-castle, more modest in size but filled with reminders of the time of the Monroe Doctrine and containing reminders of visits to Europe during the reign of Napoleon. And, perhaps, there could be no more appropriate place for a print of the Emanuel Leutze painting, "Washington Crossing the Delaware," in which there stands behind Washington a young 18-year-old, Lt. James Monroe, gripping the American flag.

A visit to Charlottesville provides a reminder that one of the nice things about our treasured places is the opportunity to walk the landscape from which history books were written.

HENNING

TENNESSEE

After the phenomenal success of his book *Roots* and the television movie based on the book, author Alex Haley had indicated he hoped someday to write a book titled *Henning*, the name of his hometown. Unfortunately, his death came too soon and deprived us of the opportunity to read the larger story of this small town.

A visit to Henning, Tennessee, is to walk among the pages of that book that was never written.

The first obvious step is the Alex Haley House and Museum, a state historic site. The house, built by Haley's grandfather in 1919, remains much as it was when Alex was a boy. This was the home of "Grandpa" Will Palmer and "Grandma" Cynthia Palmer, and became the place that housed three generations.

The front porch was the place where Alex was first bitten by what he called "the generation bug, from which there is no cure." In his Pulitzer Prize-winning *Roots*, he had written:

> . . . they had names like Aunt Plus, Aunt Liz, Aunt Till, Aunt Viney and Cousin Georgia. With the supper dishes

washed, they would go out on the front porch and sit in
cane-bottomed rocking chairs, and I would be among
them and sort of scrunch myself down behind the white-
painted rocker holding Grandma.

Haley's birth in Henning is included in the closing pages
of *Roots*. The story of *Roots,* spanning more than 600 pages,
reaches far back into his history, beginning in the early pages
with the birth of one of the story's most prominent family members, Kunta Kinte.

In one brief story Haley frames the broader meaning of the
village (or community). After witnessing the burial of his grand-
mother, the mourning and the drum beating far into the night,
Kinte was so grieved that he hardly ate or slept. One evening
his father took him into the hut and:

> . . . speaking to his son far more softly and gently than he
> ever had before, told him something that helped to ease
> his grief.

> He said that three groups of people lived in every village.
> First were those you could see—walking around, eating,
> sleeping, and working. Second were the ancestors, whom
> Grandma Yaisa had now joined.

> "And the third people—who are they?" asked Kunta.

> "The third people," said Omoro, "are those waiting to
> be born."

Just beyond the porch, only a few steps away, is Haley's grave.
A marble slab covers the site. His name and the dates of his

birth and death are etched into the marble, and a four-word characterization: "Father, Author, Historian, Friend."

Then, the last words on the marble, a brief phrase that not only seemed to capture his view of family and community, but also his parting advice—perhaps even the subtitle for the unfinished tribute to his hometown of Henning:

Find the Good and Praise It

HOT SPRINGS

ARKANSAS

The people of Hot Springs, Arkansas, didn't have to spend any time working on a name for their city. After all, about a million gallons of the 143-degree water pours out of the ground each day from 47 springs.

As early as 1832, the special properties of the area were recognized by the government, and Congress established the first federally protected area in the nation's history. (Hot Springs National Park was subsequently established in 1921.) Today the park covers more than 5,000 acres and surrounds the north end of the city.

But over the years, there have been other names—the Native Americans called it "the Valley of Vapors" and there was an era when the nickname "The American Spa" was in popular use.

National and even international visitors stayed for weeks to receive therapeutic baths.

According to legend, in 1886 A.G. Spalding and Cap Anson brought their Chicago White Stockings baseball team to Hot Springs and the tradition of spring training began. Over the years, many of the best-known names of baseball came to town—Babe Ruth visited nine times in preparation for approaching seasons. He developed a regimen of mountain hikes, golf and hot baths. Others included Tris Speaker, Walter Johnson, Jackie Robinson, Joe Dimaggio and Hank Aaron. During his stay in Hot Springs, Honus Wagner became so involved in the community he helped coach the high school basketball team. Not only individuals but entire teams began to visit, including the Boston Red Sox, Cincinnati Reds, Brooklyn Dodgers and Philadelphia Phillies.

Many of the stories of those years are intertwined with the construction of ball fields, which no longer exist, and hotels, which have been renovated. Two such stories are part of the Babe's legend. It was in the Eastman Hotel where Ruth reportedly flipped a coin to settle his 1921 contract dispute with the New York Yankees. And in Whittington Park in 1918, Ruth reportedly hit the first 500-foot home run. It landed in a nearby alligator farm. Whittington Park is gone, but the Arkansas Alligator Farm lives on, with some 200 of the reptiles.

Today, Bathhouse Row, the largest existing collection of 20th-century bathhouses in the U.S., proudly carries the designation of a National Historic Landmark. The bathhouses were designed in keeping with the European spas in the early 1900s. Major renovation efforts of the buildings on Bathhouse Row were begun in the 1990s, and continued into the beginning of the 21st century.

The citizenry is restoring and reviving its heritage by the downtown landmarks, refreshing the Victorian architecture and reclaiming its identity as evidenced by the phrase boldly spread across the website—"America's First Resort."

Visitors are coming at the rate of 1.5 million per year.

KEY WEST

FLORIDA

Key West is as far south as you can go in the U.S., which makes it a unique place to escape. The attraction and charm is its openness and acceptance of residents and visitors with a spectrum of interests and lifestyles, including elegant art galleries, literary festivals and large villas, as well as offbeat parades and a continuous happy hour. It is a port of call for cruise ships and the home of artists as well as those whose lives are traditional but enjoy the wonders of this community with a rich history, great weather and opportunities to experience nature's wonders. In brief, it is a place with multiple appeals.

What is particularly intriguing about Key West is its historic evolution and often dramatic transformations, directly linked to its location. A critical naval location for shipping and defense, it also has depended on fishing, wrecking and salvaging of sunken ships, salt production, turtling, sponge production and cigar manufacturing. (At one point Key West had 133 cigar factories.)

Along with its climate, each economic evolution has added to its mystique, creating a city unique in America.

President Harry Truman made it his "Summer White House" with many of his successors using it as an R and R destination. Ernest Hemmingway had a "grand house" in the Old Town section of Key West at the same time Tennessee Williams lived in a modest bungalow in the "unfashionable" part of the city. It has been the setting for movies, television series and the subject of songs, including Jimmy Buffett's "Margaritaville" as well as the home of famous musicians, writers, philosophers, actors, athletes and treasure hunters.

Symbolic of its residents' passion for their city was a Don Quixote-esque effort to create the Conch Republic and secede from the U.S., along with a now-restrained tradition of letting chickens walk freely throughout the city.

Few locations of its size provide the breadth and mix of historic, recreational, environmental and quirky attractions as Key West, whether biking, kayaking in a mangrove swamp, or watching the sunset in Mallory Square. Other attractions include visiting museums, art galleries the Key West Naval Air Station, and experiencing the unrestrained revelry on Duval Street.

Key West is a city with appeal for people with disparate interests, lifestyles, curiosity and a bit of adventure. It is truly unique and that, in itself, makes it worth experiencing.

.... ◯◞ ....

In his memoirs titled *A Moveable Feast*, Hemingway wrote about another place where he had lived: "If you are lucky enough to have lived in Paris as a young man, then wherever you go for the rest of your life, it stays with you, for Paris is a moveable feast."

While the statement is highly complimentary of Paris, it also can serve in an aspirational way for all citizens: to build their community in such a way that their young men and women will always remember their hometown as "a moveable feast."

OXFORD

MISSISSIPPI

With the donation of 50 acres of land, the location was established. And from the very beginning, the early settlers had a vision. In general, this would be a town centered on education. Specifically, the goal was to become the home of the first state university in Mississippi.

The name of the town was chosen in keeping with the vision, Oxford, after the university town in England.

Oxford, Mississippi, was founded in 1837. Four years later, in 1841, the Mississippi Legislature voted to locate its first university there.

The future was bright. But as the clouds of the Civil War grew darker, Oxford's darkest day was April 22, 1864, when the city was engulfed in flames. "Oxford was destroyed. There were no more businesses, supply depots, warehouses, no courthouse, and nearly every house in the area was torched."

The rebuilding began, slowly. By 1872, a new courthouse was built on the old courthouse square.

Another battle emerged, except this time the foe was Yellow Fever, taking 70 lives in 1898.

As the new century began, new families came to Oxford. In 1902 Murray Falkner (the spelling was changed later to *Faulkner*) moved his family to Oxford and worked at the university. It was the beginning of a long and famous relationship between his son William and the city of Oxford.

Perhaps as many as 15 of William Faulkner's novels are set in Mississippi. The fictional town is Jefferson, but surely Oxford was in his mind, and the county of Lafayette becomes Yoknapatawpha County, an imaginary region with a Chickasha name, which according to Faulkner means "water flows slow through flat land." (Faulkner even provided a map locating fictional places and events from his novels.)

Over the years, Faulkner received the National Book Award for Fiction in 1951 and 1955, the Pulitzer Prize for Fiction (1955 and 1963) and the Nobel Prize in Literature in 1949.

It seems perfectly appropriate that a city, which from the beginning has placed a high value on education, should enjoy such local literary success.

And the citizens of Oxford continue to celebrate literary art and artists. Each April they host the Oxford Conference of the Book. In June and July there's the Faulkner and Yoknapatawpha Conference. And located on the historic square is an independent bookstore in three separate buildings. Square Books, founded in 1979, was named Bookstore of the Year in 2013 by *Publishers Weekly*.

We especially enjoyed the opportunity to spend some time at Rowan Oak, William Faulkner's House, which is now maintained as a National Historic Landmark. This was the home for Faulkner and his family until his death in 1962, and the place where he did most of his writing. Especially memorable is the wall of his study, on which remain the handwritten outlined notes from which he wrote his Pulitzer Prize-winning novel *A Fable*.

When Faulkner traveled to Stockholm, Sweden, to receive the Nobel Prize, his acceptance speech included the following:

> . . . he (man) has a soul, a spirit capable of compassion and sacrifice and endurance. The poet's, the writer's, duty is to write about these things. It is his privilege to help man endure by lifting his heart, by reminding him of the courage and honor and hope and pride and compassion and pity and sacrifice which have been the glory of his past.

When he returned from Sweden with the $30,000 cash prize, Faulkner used the money to set up a fund for good works in his hometown.

ROCK HILL

SOUTH CAROLINA

Leadership matters in sustaining and building a city. And the continuity of creative and aligned leadership over time can promote a humane culture, engaged citizens and the physical infrastructure of a great city. There is no better example of such a community than Rock Hill, South Carolina.

Today it has become one of, if not the, cycling hub in America with a world-class velodrome (track cycling), with BMX Supercross and mountain bike trails and a criterium— closed road course for competitive racing. This is just the most recent transformation of this city, one that not only developed to serve the citizens of the community, but also an economic engine that draws cycle enthusiasts from around the world.

For more than 100 years Rock Hill was a prosperous mill town, one that was compelled to confront the scourge of segregation and economic decline, beginning in the late 1960s and 1970s. Plants closed down, retail sales declined and downtown businesses were forced to close, and the Civil Rights Movement exposed the gaping disparities between white and black. While there were those who resisted change, a new group of leaders, both elected officials and appointed managers, took steps to transform the community.

Unlike virtually all South Carolina cities, Rock Hill took advantage of the federal monies available to address the economic and social challenges of distressed communities. Beginning with the funding of a Model Cities program, Rock Hill sought out and leveraged federal monies to "update infrastructure in the entire city . . . and also paid for programs that would begin to heal the scars of racial inequality and segregation." It was argued that during the 1970s, Rock Hill recognized the opportunities provided through federal programs and received more federal monies than the rest of South Carolina cities combined.

Officials took risks, generated public support, and redefined the character of engagement and civic opportunities. A series of inspiring leaders promoted significant public and private investment and created a culture of citizen participation. The investment in major park development generated significant controversy with a leading supporter, Doug Echols, who was voted out of office as a member of the City Council. He later ran for mayor and has been instrumental in building on the expansion of the city's recreation facilities, among other initiatives, as a resource for residents and a magnet for competitive soccer tournaments and an engine for sports tourism.

Strategically recognizing the potential interest in cycling, the newest iteration of sports tourism has been the development of the rich mix of cycling venues and expanding the city's reputation as the center for cycling in the United States. In 2016 Rock Hill hosted, among other events, the Union Cycliste Internationale (UCI) BMX World Supercross World Cup with more than 200 international pro-elite cyclists. In

2017 it hosted the UCI BMX World Championships and an estimated 3,300 cyclists from around the world.

For cycling enthusiasts and those who are unfamiliar with the enormous range of cycling programs for the competitive and recreational bikers, there is no place offering more than Rock Hill.

ST. AUGUSTINE

FLORIDA

The city of St. Augustine celebrated its 450th birthday on September 8, 2015.

It is the oldest permanent European settlement on the North American continent, 42 years older than Jamestown, Virginia, and 55 years ahead of Plymouth Rock, Massachusetts.

The settlement was the result of an effort of King Phillip of Spain to establish an early presence in the new land. The king's top explorer, Don Pedro Menendez de Aviles, landed on the Florida coast on August 28, 1565, the Feast Day of St. Augustine. The city's name was chosen to honor Saint Augustine of Hippo, a fourth-century writer in philosophy and theology.

A walk along the streets of St. Augustine is literally a walk through a story spanning five centuries. A story of the diversity of times and peoples, tangibles and intangibles, of land and sea, old and new, artfully combined in an ever changing grand collage of community.

A few illustrations follow, passing through the centuries:

1675—Castillo de San Marcos

The National Park Service information opens in the following way:

> America Begins Here—A monument not only of stone and mortar but of human determination and endurance, the Castillo de San Marcos symbolizes the clash between cultures which ultimately resulted in our uniquely unified nation.

Before 1675 there had been other forts, all made of wood. Each had been destroyed by outside forces. But Castillo de San Marcos was built using coquina stone, a unique substance comprised of sand and small seashells, quarried from nearby Anastasia Island. The stone itself has a light and porous nature, rather unusual for a fortress wall and was apparently used because of its ready availability. Somewhat surprisingly, it proved highly effective when, under attack by cannon balls, the walls did not shatter or break. Their porous nature allowed cannon balls to penetrate the coquina stone and be absorbed. The walls continue to stand as, according to the National Park Service information, "the only extant 17th-century military construction in the country and the oldest masonry fortress in the United States."

1749—The Avero House was added to the U.S. National Register of Historic Places in 1972, but is known as the St. Photios Greek Orthodox National Shrine, dedicated to the first colony of Greek people who came to America. A chapel features Byzantine décor and a museum contains exhibits and information about the early Greek settlers.

1824—St. Augustine is the site of the oldest permanent aid to navigation in North America. The first official light was lit in an "Old Spanish Watchtower" in May 1824. Improvements continued over the following years, including the addition of a hand-blown, 9-foot-tall Fresnel lens from Paris, France, in 1874. The ravages of the sea and the storms eventually brought the lighthouse down. But in the 1980s the community rallied to restore the lighthouse and add a museum. Visitors can climb the 219 steps to enjoy a beautiful view of St. Augustine and its surroundings from 165 feet above sea level. University students spend the summer in museum-organized underwater archaeology school, in scientific diving among hundreds of documented shipwrecks. And the museum welcomes more than 200,000 visitors each year.

1888—The anticipated transition into the 20th century was marked by the opening of the 540-room Hotel Ponce de Leon. Henry Flagler, a major influence in the development of the Florida east coast, saw the town transition from sand and shell-covered roads to the arrival of his Jacksonville, St. Augustine & Halifax Railroad.

The majestic Gilded Age resort hotel closed in 1967 and reopened the next year as Flagler College, maintaining its distinctive and influential presence in the community.

Some 20 years after the hotel opening, Flagler reflected:

Here was St. Augustine, the oldest city in the United States. How to build a hotel to meet the requirements of nineteenth-century America and have it in keeping with the character of the place—that was my hardest problem.

1920s—The Bridge of Lions was originally built in the mid-1920s to replace the wooden bridge to Anastasia Island which dated back to the 1890s. But the idea was for the new bridge to be something more than an aid to transportation. It was to be a work of art, a landmark of note. The plan was successful.

Today, the Bridge of Lions is listed on the National Register of Historic Places and has become something of a "photographic signature" of the nation's oldest city.

The name for the bridge came from a citizen of St. Augustine, Dr. Andrew Anderson, who believed it was important to have works of art in public places and arranged for two marble Medici lion statues to be made in Florence, Italy, and positioned strategically on the bridge.

As St. Augustine entered the 21st century, the need for improvements on the almost 80-year-old bridge became obvious. The bridge was closed for rehabilitation in 2006 and the lions were placed in safer confines until they returned in 2011, marking the completion of the renovation.

The lions are named "Firm" and "Faithful," characteristics of the beautiful bridge upon which they proudly stand—and also a tribute to the residents of this city, who refuse to yield to the vicissitudes of age, preferring instead to perpetrate life and beauty.

⌣

A city is the greatest work of art possible
—Lloyd Rees, Australian artist

TUSCUMBIA

ALABAMA

Tuscumbia was actually the third name given to this town located in the northwestern corner of Alabama. In about 1780, it was a trading post near the Tennessee River named "Ococoposa," the Chickasaw word meaning "cold water." By 1817 it was called Big Spring and in 1822 the settlers named it in honor of Chief Tuscumbia, a Chickasaw rainmaker.

It was on June 27, 1880, that Helen Keller was born in Tuscumbia and her name, and her story, have been celebrated in this community since that day.

Ivy Green, Keller's childhood home, was built in 1820 and is listed in the National Register of Historic Places. Inside the house are hundreds of her personal mementos from her travels across America and throughout the world on behalf of the blind and the deaf-blind. Keller was the first deaf-blind person to earn a Bachelor of Arts degree, and her Braille books library and Braille typewriter can be found there.

The nicely landscaped grounds surrounding the house provide an elaboration of Keller's story, including the outdoor kitchen, the carriage house, a memorial fountain and the well pump where she and her teacher, Anne Sullivan, made a memorable communication breakthrough with the word "water."

Her story, so well told in William Gibson's *The Miracle Worker*, as a dramatic play and motion picture, is performed on the grounds of Ivy Green during June and July of each year.

In the mid-1970s, also during the month of June, the citizens of Tuscumbia began a multi-day celebration of their famous citizen each year, drawing as many as 50,000 people. The Helen Keller Festival pays tribute to "America's First Lady of Courage."

The Spring 2017 issue of *LEAN* magazine contained an article titled "Tuscumbia's Helen Keller: An Enduring Legacy." Sarah J. Schmidt suggested that anyone "searching for inspiration need look no further than the charming north Alabama town of Tuscumbia, site of Helen Keller's birthplace and host of the annual celebration that honors her amazing life."

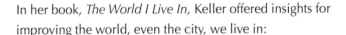

In her book, *The World I Live In,* Keller offered insights for improving the world, even the city, we live in:

> The only lightless dark is the night of ignorance and insensibility. We differ, blind and seeing, one from another, not in our senses, but in the use we make of them, in the imagination and courage with which we seek wisdom beyond our senses.

TUSKEGEE

ALABAMA

In 1881, Tuskegee Normal School was founded on a former plantation. The director of the school was Booker T. Washington, who devoted himself to what is now known as Tuskegee University, believing that education was the key to improving one's life. Washington was one of the most influential African-American leaders of the late 19th and early 20th century. An impressive sculpture depicting him is now located prominently on the Tuskegee campus. The inscription at the base of the monument honors his impact in the way he "pointed the way to progress through education and industry."

In 1896, George Washington Carver was invited to join the Tuskegee faculty as head of the agriculture department. For more than 40 years, Carver taught methods of farming and crop rotation, while researching and experimenting with peanuts, sweet potatoes and other crops. As his reputation grew, he spent more of his time speaking, writing and meeting with, among others, three U.S. presidents.

Carver was buried next to Washington on the campus of Tuskegee University. On Carver's gravestone are these words:

"He could have added fortune to fame, but caring for neither, he found happiness and honor in being helpful to the world."

In 1923, the Tuskegee Veterans Administration Medical Center was established for an estimated 300,000 African-American veterans of World War I.

In 1940 to 1942, Moton Field was built to provide primary flight training for the U.S. military. The first squadron of African-American pilots were trained there for service in World War II, known as the Tuskegee Airmen. The field was named for Robert Russa Moton, the second president of Tuskegee University.

In 2012, American singer, songwriter and producer Lionel Richie released an album with the title "Tuskegee," his hometown. He surely had heard the stories of Washington and Carver and the Tuskegee Airmen. In the album jacket he eloquently reflected on the impact a community, its people and their stories has on each emerging generation:

Every soul has a birth place,
every dream starts somewhere.
My life, my adventures, my destiny
my music and the truth of who I am
all started in this one place called,
Tuskegee.
—Lionel Richie

WILLIAMSBURG

VIRGINIA

Williamsburg, Virginia, is a city with its colonial past providing a living history museum/experience at its center. Colonial Williamsburg has created an opportunity for total immersion into an earlier era where "the future may learn from the past," and where visitors can engage with costumed employees to learn about "their" lives, perceptions, daily challenges, work and hopes. It is a city that has taken its historic roots to define itself.

The 301-acre historic area is an "interpretation of a colonial American city" combining the restoration of historic buildings and recreation of streets that "attempts to suggest the atmosphere and the circumstances of 18th-century America."

Founded in 1638, Williamsburg was the first city in Virginia and the wealthiest of the early American colonies, home of the College of William and Mary and Eastern Lunatic Asylum (now Eastern State Hospital). It was said in the 1700s that the "500 Crazies of the asylum supported the 500 Lazies of the college and town." Until 1780, Williamsburg was the center of government, education and culture in the Colony of Virginia. When Gov. Thomas Jefferson moved the capital of

Virginia to Richmond, Williamsburg went through a period of "sleepy stagnation and decay which by the 20th century much of the older historical buildings were destroyed or in poor condition."

In the 1920s, the financial support and leadership of John D. Rockefeller Jr., his wife, Abby, and other individuals and organizations created the foundation that purchased the land and began restoring and recreating Colonial Williamsburg. This philanthropic initiative acknowledged the remarkable historic asset of the city and established it along with the College of William and Mary as the defining economic anchors for Williamsburg.

In Williamsburg, "tourists are not just outsiders looking in—they are temporary citizens experiencing the Revolutionary City as it was in the 18th century." It is possible to take advantage of an orientation offered by Colonial Williamsburg, follow a well-planned visitors program or simply walk the Duke of Gloucester Street to explore "living" historic buildings, visit with costumed "citizens" or respond to the diversions of the moment, including a Haunted Tour of Williamsburg, a day in court at the Capitol, or locking up family members in the stocks.

Williamsburg is but one point in this historic triangle in Virginia. The others include Jamestown—the first English settlement established 13 years before the Pilgrims landed in Plymouth Rock, where visitors can tour a Powhatan Indian village and a 17th-century fort.

The third point on the triangle is historic Yorktown and the Yorktown Battlefield, where George Washington's victory ended the Revolutionary War. While these historic offerings define the area, there are many other attractions for visitors including the College of William and Mary, and the Busch Gardens theme park, which might well be the carrot parents use to lure their skeptical children to experience Colonial Williamsburg.

This is a city that recognized the significance of its history and created an opportunity for visitors to experience how the "future may learn from the past."

LEARNING FROM OTHERS

DON BORUT

Education doesn't end with the receipt of a diploma. Life experience, reading, interaction with others, travel, attendance at events, meetings and conferences all expand the way we continue to learn, grow and improve our ability to more effectively operate and, ideally, improve the quality of our lives.

A major responsibility of the two national local government associations with which I worked, the International City/County Management Association (ICMA) and the National League of Cities (NLC), was to bring together local government officials to share information, ideas and programs for the purpose of improving the effectiveness, efficiency and quality of local public services.

Local elected officials with whom I worked ran for public office for many different reasons: to make a contribution, respond to a specific problem or a community crisis, follow a desire to serve, answer a plea or request from a friend, or fulfill a personal need and/or a specific passion for an issue or some broader undefined objective. No matter the motivation, virtually every person with whom I worked sincerely believed in and was committed to improving their communities. I might have questioned how they approached their role or even their underlying motivation, but they genuinely believed and wanted to make what they felt was a positive contribution to their community, and they wanted to be respected and appreciated for their efforts. This last point should not be discounted or denigrated. It is a basic human characteristic that makes their efforts and contributions no less important and valuable.

Through the National League of Cities, local elected officials are able to engage with colleagues who are addressing similar programmatic challenges with diverse constituencies and the need to make decisions that affect the daily lives of citizens. Through meetings, workshops and conferences focused on specific issues, e.g. from infrastructure, police community relations, and economic development, mayors and council members are able to engage with each other, not as partisans but as colleagues. It is often observed that there isn't a Republican or Democratic way to fill a pothole. Perspectives may have been different, but these officials are not driven by ideology. By necessity, they are pragmatic realists.

Another way local officials learned from each other was to visit other cities to see programs in place, to truly understand not only what was accomplished but also how it was implemented. A number of cities organized trips to a different city each year to see a project or program that was directly relevant to their community. NLC purposely held its meetings in different cities for members to have the opportunity to be exposed to different operations, programs and, frankly, municipal cultures.

An interesting challenge I confronted at ICMA and NLC was how to share information about a program or initiative that didn't work. In many ways, so-called failures can be more important in terms of understanding the unintended consequences of a particular initiative. In the informal, off-the-record environment of meetings or informal discussions, both city managers and local elected officials were willing to be candid with each other, but few if any were prepared to describe these unsuccessful initiatives in writing. Risk taking in the public sector is difficult regardless how necessary it is in order to bring about change. More than in the private sector, there is always someone or some group ready to find fault with any public decision or action.

In an attempt to address this reality, ICMA explored an idea proposed by a California city manager, Ed Everett. It was to create an award to recognize "Fabulous Flops." In brief, it used humor to tease out programs that were not successful and thus provide a way for managers to describe a program using an element of self-deprecation that generated respect for the effort and the author.

To me, the benefit of learning about creative programs, specifically by visiting other cities, seems self-evident. However, I was often perplexed when I heard from officials that they didn't see any reason to attend conferences or visit other communities. Equally disconcerting was citizen criticism when their mayors or council members attended conferences or visited other cities, referring to these trips as junkets; a waste of public funds. In public speeches I would often ask audiences if it was a junket for their doctor or dentist to participate in programs to improve their ability to better serve their patients. Learning by experiencing, and understanding new and alternative strategies for dealing with an issue are fundamental to expanding the ability to better serve individual patients as well as the citizens of a community.

Visiting other cities also can be a wonderful learning opportunity for individuals and families. It is a way to understand and appreciate the breadth, range, and diversity of the unique cities in our nation. And it provides the joy of discovery.

TREASURED PLACES

OF THE

CENTRAL
UNITED STATES

ABILENE

TEXAS

A bilene has a history of civic leadership and boosterism reflected in the transformative initiatives beginning in the 1880s, when the Texas and Pacific Railroad needed a stopping point across West Texas. The deep roots of cowboys and cattle ranchers are still celebrated with the West Texas Fair and Rodeo in the fall and the Western Heritage Classic in the spring. But today, Abilene is the vibrant cultural hub of West Texas, known as the Big Country or the Texas Midwest, with an impressive number of colleges and universities for a city its size and a major military facility, Dyess Air Force Base, established as a result of proactive civic leadership.

Like many cities, Abilene saw a decline in its downtown but as in the past, benefited from aligned civic leaders who generated support for a sales tax dedicated to economic development. The result was a significant downtown restoration, the preservation and restoration of a historic hotel into the Grace Museum, an art and cultural center, and the restoration of a 1930 movie house into the state-of-the-art Paramount Theatre, with an annual calendar of classic movies.

Frontier Texas is a multimedia museum focusing on the history of frontier life (1780 to 1880), beginning with the presence of the Comanche Indians and ending with the anticipated arrival of the railroad.

The Texas Forts Trail headquarters also is located in Frontier Texas, providing self-guided maps and information for visiting by car the sites of eight early frontier military posts, including Fort Phantom Hill, just north of Abilene.

In 1993 a children's book titled *Santa Calls* was published. The author and illustrator, William Joyce, had created a fictional adventure story about three kids who lived in Abilene, Texas. When asked why he had chosen Abilene as the location, Joyce replied that he knew nothing about Abilene except he wanted a nonfictional place in West Texas and he "liked the sound" of Abilene.

From that puzzling, yet promising beginning, Joyce was invited to Abilene to speak and to sign hundreds of his books. Out of that seed grew the National Center for Children's Illustrated Literature and the Storybook Sculpture Project, perhaps the world's largest collection of public sculptures depicting characters from children's books.

It also has inspired, among other events, the Children's Art and Literacy Festival each June. Combined with the long-standing West Texas Book Festival in September, the result for Abilene is what one writer has described as the "book festival capital of Texas," and the Texas Legislature has officially named Abilene the "Storybook Capital of Texas."

This is a city that speaks to and serves the interests and needs of its citizens while serving as a magnet for readers beyond its borders, drawn by the magic allure of stories that come alive and excite the imagination.

The well-known characters of Dr. Seuss, among the other bronze sculptures in downtown Abilene, stand as a continuing reminder, to all residents of all their hometowns, of the familiar Seussical saying,

> Unless someone like you cares a whole awful lot,
> Nothing is going to get better. It's not.
> —from *The Lorax*

BARTLESVILLE

OKLAHOMA

Before it was Bartlesville, it was Bartles Town, the name derived from Jacob Bartles, son-in-law of the Delaware chief, Charles Journeycake. Bartles had moved from Kansas into this part of Indian Territory (Osage, Cherokee, Delaware) in the mid-1870s to open a trading post and post office.

In 1897 the population of Bartlesville was about 200, when two oil entrepreneurs, George Keeler and William Johnstone, are credited with igniting an oil boom in Oklahoma that continues to boost the state economy to this day. At 3 p.m. on April 15, 1897, the Nellie Johnstone No. 1 blew in as a gusher, producing 50-75 barrels of oil a day. It took two years to establish the necessary storage and transportation system to accommodate such a supply but by May 1900 oil was successfully shipped at $1.25 per barrel.

The Nellie Johnstone No. 1 produced more than 100,000 barrels in its lifetime and the population of Bartlesville exploded from 200 to 4,000 in a 10-year period.

Today, a replica derrick of the well stands on the original site just north of downtown Bartlesville on Cherokee Avenue.

In 1904, two brothers from Iowa, Frank and L.E. Phillips, came to Bartlesville, drilled their first wildcat well and struck oil in June 1905. A few dry holes followed, and then, almost out of funds, they hit a gusher, known as the Anna Anderson No. 1, the first of 80 straight producing oil wells— and the beginning of what in 1917 would become Phillips Petroleum Company.

A visitor to Bartlesville today will enjoy an excellent experience in the Phillips Petroleum Company Museum, which tells a story of the oil industry, from the small beginning of discovery to the global expansion of the 21st century.

To capture a more complete picture of the oil boom days and the man who was a major part of the story, the Frank Phillips Home, a National Register Historic Site, has been preserved by the Oklahoma Historical Society, including its family heirlooms and furnishings.

Two other places are important to understanding the Bartlesville story: Woolaroc and Claremore.

Back in 1905, when the Phillips brothers first struck oil, there was another native Oklahoma boy experiencing a breakthrough in an entirely different way. After developing a reputation as a "lasso artist" in Wild West shows, Will Rogers made his way to New York and in 1905 performed in a horse show in Madison Square Garden. His roping skills, combined with his Western drawl, were so well received that he stayed in New York, working in vaudeville.

His career as an entertainer was launched, but he returned to Oklahoma to establish his home base, buying a 20-acre tract of land in Claremore, about 45 miles from Bartlesville.

Rogers and Phillips became neighbors and good friends. Woolaroc, the country estate of Frank Phillips, located some

12 miles outside of Bartlesville, is a combination wildlife preserve and museum housing more than 55,000 pieces of fine art and relics, lending beauty and authenticity to the story of the American West.

"When you are visiting the beauty spots of this country," Rogers said, "don't overlook Frank Phillips' ranch and game preserve. . . . It's the most unique place in this country."

Today, Claremore is the home of the Will Rogers Memorial Museum. Rogers, known as "Oklahoma's Favorite Son," continued to gain fame with a rope act in the Ziegfield Follies and at his untimely death, had a highly popular radio program, a newspaper column read by millions and more than 70 movies to his credit. The museum, where we found we could easily spend half the day, houses, in addition to memorabilia and manuscripts, a theater featuring his films.

But Will Rogers is remembered more for his quotes than his columns or movies. And one of his perhaps less-known quotes supports the idea of this book:

> You would be surprised what there is to see in this great country within 200 miles of where any of us live. I don't care what state or what town.

COLUMBUS

INDIANA

Place matters in defining who we are, enhancing our quality of life and how we feel about our community. Many factors contribute to creating place—values, culture, leadership, urban design and the built environment, among others. On the last, Winston Churchill observed that "we shape our buildings: thereafter they shape us." Columbus, Indiana, personifies the profound impact building design—architecture—can have in contributing to the quality of life of a community.

According to architecture critic Blair Kamin, Columbus is "a small-town architectural mecca." "With more than 60 notable buildings and monuments, Columbus is the nation's sixth most architecturally significant city, behind Chicago, New York, San Francisco, Boston and Washington D.C., according to the American Institute of Architects.

A small Midwestern industrial city, Columbus' appreciation and commitment to quality architecture were not evolutionary: rather it was the vision, inspiration and leadership of J. Irwin Miller, chair and CEO of Cummins Engine. "He wanted to help the community by providing an alternative to the standard, but uninspired school buildings being built at a rapid pace across the U.S. in the late 1950s and early 1960s."

Miller wrote:

> Every one of us lives and moves all his life within the limitations, sight and influence of architecture—at home, at school, at church and at work. The influences of architecture with which we are surrounded in our youth affects our lives, our standards, our tastes when we are grown, just as the influence of parents and teachers with which we are surrounded in our youth affects us as adults.

In 1957 he engaged with city officials and agreed to pay architecture fees if the city would commission first-rate designers. By the 1970s great architecture became part of Columbus' civic DNA and the catalyst for enriching and mobilizing citizen, civic and business engagement and commitment to the city.

The work of the world's leading architects is embedded in the fabric of the community, including schools, the city hall, the adult education center, Streetscapes, the county library and the Solid Waste District Board (landfill). The works of the giants of 20th century Modernism, including I.M. Pei, Eero Saarinen, Cesar Pelli, Richard Meier, Edward Charles Beeby, Deborah Berke, John M. Johansen, Paul Kennon, Robert Venturi and more are present in Columbus.

Inspiring architecture is clearly the unique and defining characteristic which is the basis of Columbus' national and international reputation, but there is much more to the city that defines the quality of life for its residents and makes it a magnet for visitors. Architecture has been a catalyst providing leverage for economic development as well a rich cultural and arts base, as reflected in numerous articles written about the city and the awards it has received.

Fortune Small Business magazine ranked Columbus in the top 100 "Best Places to Live and Launch" a business. *USA Today* included the city in "10 great places to discover Midwest charm." It has a diverse schedule of community events, including bluegrass, pop, art, Scottish heritage, ethnic cuisine and culture, and symphonic performances. And few places have been as systematic in facilitating the engagement of visitors as Columbus through bus tours, step-on guide services, extended architecture tours, downtown walking tours, video presentations, and exhibits.

DULUTH

MINNESOTA

In the late 1800s, Duluth, Minnesota, was called the "Zenith City of the Unsalted Seas." When the Sault Ste. Marie canal opened, Duluth became the only port able to access both the Atlantic and Pacific oceans because of its connections to the west. By 1869, Duluth was considered the fastest growing city in the U.S.

The Duluth-Superior harbor on the north shore of Lake Superior is the region's largest port and the westernmost point of the Freshwater Great Lakes. The Atlantic lies more than 2,000 miles to the east.

As the industrial component of the U.S. economy began to wane in the 1950s, changes became necessary. Old warehouses were converted or replaced along the shoreline of Lake Superior.

The spirit of the Zenith City remains undaunted as more than 3 million visitors per year visit the new Canal Park area, adding some $400 million to the local economy.

The transformation is an impressive blending of visible reminders of the past (such as retrofitted restaurants inside former warehouses) with a fresh new presence of hotels, shops and recreation along a four-mile-long Lakewalk. The historic Aerial Lift Bridge is still there, looming large on the horizon, and the new Great Lakes Aquarium opened in 2000, featuring animals and habitats as near as the Great Lakes Basin and as distant as the Amazon River.

And in keeping with its long-held identity, North America's largest sturgeon touch tank opened to the aquarium in this Zenith City—and it's named "Unsalted Seas."

Most of our afternoon was spent along the Lakewalk, viewing the remarkable results of the very extensive renewal project. A small sign provided an insight into the intentionality behind the transformation: "One vital component of this revitalization program was to commission seven major works of art to be incorporated into the Canal Park area." More than $200,000 was dedicated to sponsoring a national competition from artists' proposals.

One of the winners was Douglas Freeman, whose sculpture, "Fountain of the Wind," is an intriguing interactive "poem of honor, respect and gratitude," a composition of bronze, stainless steel and glass in lasting tribute to Lake Superior.

Almost as a magnet, the sculpture draws people together in the midst of this reimagined yet historical area. The children step from stone to stone across the waters within the sculpture.

And Freeman's words about his sculpture are true for the entire area: "The sculpture tells no single story. The stories are yours to tell."

DURANGO

COLORADO

Durango was established in 1881 by the Denver and Rio Grande Railroad to serve the mining industry in the San Juan Mountains, which in 1860 had been the area of the first gold rush in southwestern Colorado. A railroad line was built to Silverton and is still in service today as a popular tourist attraction.

The Durango & Silverton Narrow Gauge Railroad (D&SNG) has been operating on 45 miles of track from Durango to Silverton since 1881, and is one of the few places to operate steam locomotives continuously. The D&SNG is listed as a National Historic Landmark.

In the winter of 2016, a new and creative role for the railroad was added. Children and families are invited for a "Polar Express" adventure, based on the popular award-winning book by Chris Van Allsburg. As if they are living into the story, children are encouraged to board the train still wearing their pajamas and enjoy hot chocolate while riding the train to pick up Santa and return to Durango.

In the process, the 1881 railroad has been given new life once more—from carrying freight, to historic tourism, to childhood adventure.

But the train is not the only historic magnet, nor the oldest in the Durango area. Thirty-nine miles away is Mesa Verde National Park, the site of hundreds of well-preserved ancestral Pueblo cliff dwellings. Dating back to 1190, these pueblos were built beneath overhanging cliffs. Because of its exceptional archaeological relevance, Mesa Verde (Spanish for green table) was named a national park by President Theodore Roosevelt in 1906.

It was designated a World Heritage Site in 1978, one of only 23 such recognitions in the nation. Comments contained in the World Heritage Site designation include: "Within the boundaries of the property are located all the elements necessary to understand and express the Outstanding Universal Value of Mesa Verde National Park. . . . Large portions of the sandstone and mud-mortar multi-story buildings have survived intact in form and materials, a tribute to the engineering skills of these early peoples as well as the dry environment of the mesa's alcoves."

The natural beauty of the extreme southwestern corner of Colorado is in itself an attraction. The rugged beauty, even in the name of the Rocky Mountains, combined with flowing blue waters that attracts campers, hikers and especially fishermen to the Animas River (meaning water of the soul), combine to create a setting for a town named Durango. The name was borrowed from Durango, Mexico (established in 1563), which borrowed it from Durango, Spain (established in the 13th century), and the word originates from a Bosque word *wrango*, meaning *water town*, or perhaps, town by the water.

The Durango surroundings look as if they could be a setting for a motion picture which, in fact, they have been. More than 30 films have used the landscapes and the railroad for their locations. Perhaps the best remembered scene is from *Butch Cassidy and the Sundance Kid,* when Paul Newman and Robert Redford made their famous leap off the cliff and into the waters just outside Durango.

In addition to the Sundance Kid, there was another "kid" who borrowed the town's name for his identity. In 1940, Charles Starrett was cast in the starring role of *The Durango Kid*. Five years later, *The Return of the Durango Kid* was released and a generation of loyal fans supported an ongoing series eventually totaling 65 Durango Kid films. The final one, *The Kid From Broken Gun,* was produced in 1952. Collections of the classic's black and white films continue to be viewed by a new generation of fans.

FREDERICKSBURG

TEXAS

The early years of Fredericksburg tell the story of German immigration. Founded in 1846 under the leadership of Baron John Meusebach, the commissioner general of the Society for the Protection of German Immigrants in Texas, the immigrants were fleeing the difficult conditions in Germany that later resulted in the Revolution of 1848.

The decision was made to settle in a valley in the Texas Hill Country between two gentle-flowing streams today known as Barons Creek (in honor of the town's founder) and Town Creek. Fredericksburg was named in honor of Prince Frederick of Prussia.

Within a year, an estimated 600 people had built log houses along both sides of the main street, and many huts of clay and moss dotted the expanding area.

If there is one day best representing the transformation of this quiet, close-knit community of immigrants into a perennially popular destination that now finds tourism to be a major factor in the local economy, perhaps it would be April 16, 1961.

On that day, U.S. Vice President Lyndon Johnson, joined by Fleet Admiral Chester Nimitz and West Germany

Chancellor Konrad Adenauer, stepped out of a helicopter onto the Fredericksburg fairgrounds. The town's population was then slightly under 5,000, but the crowd approached 10,000. Johnson and Nimitz spoke in English, Adenauer and other speakers, in German. But it was reported that translators were not needed for this audience.

Today, the sidewalks and stores along that same main street, now more than 150 years old, welcome crowds of visitors every weekend of the year and every day throughout the summer.

One of the most historic sites is the National Museum of the Pacific War, the only institution in the U.S. dedicated exclusively to telling the story of the Pacific and Asiatic theaters in World War II, has now become a museum complex stretching over six acres, including the Admiral Nimitz Museum.

But Nimitz was not a visitor in 1961; he was returning to his boyhood home, a place where his grandfather, Charles Henry Nimitz, was one of those first settlers in 1846. The Admiral Nimitz Museum tells the personal story of this descendant of a German immigrant who became the U.S. commander of more than two million men and women, 5,000 ships and 20,000 planes.

Also included in the museum complex is the Plaza of Presidents, a tribute to the ten U.S. presidents who served in the military during World War II.

And the Japanese Garden of Peace is a gift from the people of Japan, a "tranquil oasis for solace and reflection" designed and constructed by Japanese craftsmen.

Fredericksburg is only about 30 miles from Johnson City, the hometown of former U.S. Vice President and then President Lyndon Johnson. The town was founded by the former president's uncle, James Polk Johnson, but gained worldwide attention as the Texas White House during the Johnson administration. During those years, national and world leaders were guests in meetings under the live oak in the front yard and at barbecue feasts by the river. The Texas White House was officially opened to the public in 2008.

In recent years, the people of Fredericksburg have added an additional identity, claiming to be second only to Napa Valley as the most visited wine region in the U.S. The Texas Hill Country Wine Region boasts of 600-plus acres of vineyards with more than 70 wineries. The road between Fredericksburg and Johnson City is U.S. Highway 290, but the 15 wineries now located along that highway prefer a new name: "Wine Road 290." Under any name, it has always been a beautiful drive through the history and heritage of the Texas Hill Country.

GALENA

ILLINOIS

The town of Galena got its name from the mineral galena, a form of lead sulfide mined along that area of the Mississippi River.

According to the *Chicago Tribune*, "By the middle of the 19th century, Galena was one of the richest river towns in the Midwest. But when the lead ran out and the river silted up, it went into a century-long decline—too poor to tear anything down. That was its salvation, and today the restored town climbing the riverside bluffs looks much like it did when Ulysses Grant worked in his father's store on Main Street. That street, with its almost solid walls of pre-Civil War buildings turned into tourist shops, is now the main attraction."

More than a million visitors a year visit Galena, population 3,460. (We spent most of a day on Main Street, as did hundreds of others.) It is not surprising that *Fodor's Travel Guide* named it one of America's Best Main Streets.

Eighty-five percent of the buildings (covering 581 acres of the city) are within the Galena Historic District, which is listed on the National Register of Historic Places. The Desoto House Hotel, named for the European discoverer of the Mississippi

River, opened in 1855 and is the "oldest operating hotel" in Illinois (guests have included Abraham Lincoln) and Grant "used rooms 209 and 211 of the hotel as his presidential campaign headquarters."

The reawakening of Galena to the tourist economy began in the 1980s and has steadily grown. Today it promotes itself as the ideal "one-tank trip" to motorists looking for a three-day vacation from the greater Chicago area.

And the efforts to redefine their town's identity have not gone unnoticed across the nation. *Forbes Traveler* named Galena one of the 10 prettiest towns in America and the National Trust for Historic Preservation listed Galena among its Dozen Distinctive Destinations in 2004.

One of the Galena distinctives is the presence of flood gates when approaching the downtown area. Because of its proximity to the Galena River (a tributary of the Mississippi River), the gates were installed in 1951 after several threats of major flood damage. As recently as 2010, while encountering an eight-inch rainfall, the flood gates were closed, preventing an estimated six inches of flood water to damage Main Street.

Galena's connection to the Civil War story was not limited to Grant. The man who later served as his Secretary of War, John Rawlins, was at one time the Galena city attorney. Ely Parker, a member of the Seneca tribe, came to Galena in the 1850s as a civil engineer, supervising government projects. While in Galena, he met Grant and later helped draft the Appomattox documents which are in his handwriting. He was the first Native American to serve as Secretary of Indian Affairs.

In 1895, to celebrate the 30th anniversary of the April 9, 1865, meeting of Lee and Grant at the Appomattox Court

House, a Thomas Nast painting titled "Peace in Union" was presented to the city of Galena.

All three of these men with Galena connections (Grant, Rawlins and Parker) were at Appomattox and are celebrated in this huge painting, which is housed in the Galena and U.S. Grant Museum.

A commemorative stamp featuring the Nast painting was issued in 2015, marking the 150th anniversary of the end of the Civil War.

The painting continues to acknowledge the way that "seeming ordinary people find the courage to do unordinary things."

Today, Galena citizens enjoy a rebirth of their community, due to their skillful efforts to protect the past while enhancing the present. The local visitors' bureau has coined a phrase to describe it: "Vintage Charm, Contemporary Spirit."

GREEN BAY

WISCONSIN

In 1934, President Franklin D. Roosevelt came to Green Bay to mark the 300th anniversary of the first trading post and small settlement created by French explorer Samuel de Chaplain's interest in forming a peaceful alliance with Native Americans to facilitate French fur trade. The location was first called *La Baye* by the French and then later became *La Baie Vert*, French for "The Green Bay."

When the Erie Canal was built in 1825, connecting New England to the Great Lakes, population growth soon followed, and the fur trade began to yield to the lumber industry. Immigrants from Europe were attracted to the jobs, particularly those from Belgium.

In Green Bay, on April 9, 1898, a young Belgian couple gave birth to a son and named him Earl Louis Lambeau. As a youth he developed an interest in sports and acquired the nickname "Curly." After a stint at Notre Dame where he played on the varsity as a freshman for coach Knute Rockne, he returned to Green Bay, working as a shipping clerk for a packing company. His love of football persisted and in 1919, he and local newspaper editor George Calhoun started a football team with $500 to buy uniforms and equipment.

Within two years the team had sufficiently proven itself and had joined the American Professional Football Association, which was soon to become the NFL. Lambeau coached the team from 1919 to 1948, during which time the Packers won 209 games and six championships.

The 1920 census listed the population of Green Bay as 31,017, making it the smallest city with an NFL team. The financial undergirding of the team had been shaky from the start and by 1922 things were grim. But that's when the relationship between the team and the town was solidified. The nonprofit Green Bay Football Corporation was formed and the Packers were owned by the community. In Green Bay the fans are not like other fans, they also are investors.

That remarkable relationship is now nearing the 100-year mark. Rick Reilly, noting that the 257th largest U.S. city has an NFL team, described it this way:

> It's like putting the United Nations in Ogallala, Nebraska. The Packers are a franchise that couldn't be, shouldn't be, but miraculously is. More than any other teams, a Packers ticket is precious.

> The club does not sell single-game tickets, which means the only way to get in, short of parachuting, is to buy a season ticket.

> If you put your name on the waiting list today, you would be number 74,659. An average of 70 people give up their tickets every year, which means you'll have your tickets by the 3074 season.

The Lambeau years with six NFL championships set a high standard. The next 15 years would yield no championships.

But things changed with the arrival of Vince Lombardi. Over nine seasons (1959-67) the Packers won five NFL championships, including Super Bowls I and II.

His was an unforgettable era for the team and the town. He seemed to have a deep insight into the similarity of qualities necessary for a team or a community to be exceptional, as he explained its essence in the following way:

> Mental toughness is humility, simplicity, Spartanism. And one other, love. . . . Love is loyalty. Love is teamwork. Love respects the dignity of the individual. Heart power is the strength of your corporation.

On practically any list of things to do in Green Bay, item number one is to visit the stadium. Two large bronze sculptures welcome visitors—Curly Lambeau and Vince Lombardi. Their lives are etched into the game of football. The stadium is Lambeau Field. The Super Bowl trophy is the Lombardi Trophy.

Reflecting on the legacy that both men have left, Travis Pipes wrote, about Lombardi,

> Ultimately, he understood that the game mattered to people, that it brought communities together, that it gave the working class a strong sense of pride. He knew what the game meant to a place like Green Bay.
>
> In many ways, Lombardi was Green Bay and Green Bay was Lombardi.

And over the years, the community of Green Bay has adopted another name:

Titletown, USA

GREENFIELD

INDIANA

Sometimes it seems that a first visit to a town follows, serendipitously, through a natural progression.

When possible, we like to begin with a search for downtown, which hopefully will provide a measure of the vitality of the community, as well as an indication of its distinctivity, or its story.

In Greenfield, the town square is easily discovered. There, in front of the courthouse, is a statue not of a government or military official, but of a former Greenfield citizen. Below the impressive statue, chiseled into the granite block, are these words:

> **JAMES WHITCOMB RILEY**
> Erected by
> American School Children

It's almost noon, and as we walk around the square, what appears to be one of the early old buildings of downtown Greenfield has been given new life, and new purpose, as an appealing contemporary restaurant. It was a fortunate choice—not only because of the Italian cuisine but also because the owner was in the dining area visiting with guests.

As he briefly joined our table, we discussed not only the story of his restaurant, but more about the story of the statue, as he suggested an additional after-lunch stop at an old but well-maintained house just a few blocks away.

The sign outside the house read:

> Birthplace
> **JAMES WHITCOMB RILEY**
> "The Hoosier Poet"
> October 7, 1849—July 22, 1916
> Editor, author, poet, lecturer and
> entertainer. One of the best known
> Hoosiers of all time.

Inside, we found the rest of the story, told by two ladies as we walked through the house filled with rooms of furniture and frames embellishing the story of Riley and his hometown.

Three stops—the statue at the courthouse square, lunch at the downtown restaurant and an old house containing a story that reaches back more than 150 years—summarized our visit to Greenfield.

And there were also four people—the author, the restaurant owner and the two women at the Riley house. They shared a common story. For each of them, Greenfield was their hometown. All of them had become ambassadors of the place where they had chosen to live. And they continue to tell the distinctive story of Greenfield.

The most essential factor is persistence—the determination
never to allow your energy or enthusiasm to be dampened
by the discouragement that must inevitably come.
—James Whitcomb Riley

HANNIBAL

MISSOURI

When John Marshall Clemens moved to Hannibal, Missouri, his son Samuel was 4 years old. Little did he know how that decision would become such a major influence in the life of his son and the life of the town.

The father became a justice of the peace, but died at the age of 49. Samuel was 11 at the time and would later write, "I was taken from school upon my father's death and placed in the office of the *Hannibal Courier*, as a printers' apprentice."

Years later, he would reflect on the early years in his hometown: "Hannibal has had a hard time of it ever since I can recollect. First, it had me for a citizen, but I was too young then to really hurt the place."

Clemens left Hannibal in 1853 at age 18, but the town has never forgotten its young citizen.

In fact, a year-long celebration in 2010 observed the 175th anniversary of Samuel Clemens' (better known as Mark Twain) birth and the 125th anniversary of *The Adventures of Huckleberry Finn*.

And the people of Hannibal have done an exemplary job of preserving the memories of Clemens' early years. A walk through the downtown area includes the Mark Twain Boyhood Home (along with the whitewashed fence), Huck Finn's house, Becky Thatcher's house, and Grant's Drugstore. Then there's the Mark Twain Cave, the Tom Sawyer and Huck Finn Statue, and a bed and breakfast including a room "where Mark Twain stayed" in his later visits.

There is also, appropriately, the Mark Twain Mississippi Riverboat, because as much as Twain's life is connected to Hannibal, it is, perhaps even more strongly, connected to the Mississippi. On April 9, 1859, 23-year-old Samuel Longhorne Clemens received his steamboat pilot's license and continued in that position until 1861, when river travel was curtailed due to Civil War hostilities. Two of his best-known books, *The Adventures of Tom Sawyer* (1876) and *The Adventures of Huckleberry Finn* (1884), are frequently recalled as "the river novels."

In between these two books, *Life on the Mississippi* was published in 1883. From his days as a steamboat river pilot, Twain wrote:

Boy after boy managed to get on the river. The minister's son became an engineer. The doctor's and the postmaster's sons became 'mud clerks'; the wholesale liquor dealer's son became a barkeeper on a boat; four sons of the chief merchant, and two sons of the county judge became pilots. Pilot was the grandest position of all. The pilot, even in those days of trivial wages, had a princely salary—from a hundred and fifty to two hundred and fifty dollars a month, and no board to pay.

One who knows the Mississippi will promptly aver—not aloud, but to himself—that ten thousand River

Commissions, with the mines of the world at their back, cannot tame that lawless stream, cannot curb it or confine it, cannot say to it, Go here, or Go there, and make it obey; . . .

Not only in 2010, but every year, Hannibal celebrates its hometown boy who William Faulkner called "The Father of American Literature."

Hannibal's citizens are skillfully keeping a unique chapter of Americana alive.

It's easy for first-time visitors to Hannibal to quickly feel they've been there before—that's probably why it seems appropriate to Hannibal to consider itself "America's Hometown" where "The Adventure of Mark Twain's day is alive and well."

INDEPENDENCE

MISSOURI

Few cities are so inextricably connected to a specific person that by mentioning the city's name, you produce his or her name.

But when I Googled "man from Independence," Harry S. Truman was the result—not once but multiple times.

Apparently, the former president would be quite comfortable with this close connection to his hometown. When he returned from his time in Washington, D.C., he explained that Independence had always been "the center of things for me."

And the citizens of Independence continue to celebrate that relationship with this favorite son. Today, the Harry S. Truman Library and Museum is located only a few blocks down the street from the Truman family home—a very walkable distance. In fact, a 2.7-mile Truman Historic Walking Trail includes 43 plaques embedded in the sidewalks through Truman's neighborhood, which would have made the namesake, known as an "incurable pedestrian," very happy.

And the visitors continue to come. Since the dedication of the Truman Presidential Library in 1957, more than 8 million have passed through the doors—and the annual visitors continue to approximate the population of Independence at 120,000.

But this city has always held an importance to travelers. Independence also is known as the Queen City of the Trails. The first overland immigrants to Oregon came in 1841 when a small group of pioneers left Independence; more followed the same course in the succeeding years and it soon was called the Oregon Trail. Similar stories are told about the role of Independence in the development of the Santa Fe Trail and the California Trail.

The starting point for these trails is marked at the site of the old courthouse building, modeled after Philadelphia's Independence Hall, in the downtown area of the city named after the Declaration of Independence.

Truman spent 64 of his 88 years in Independence. His retirement days were structured to include a morning walk, typically rising at 5:30. After perusing the morning paper but before breakfast, he strolled through the neighborhood at "a quick rate of 120 paces a minute." Along the walk, there were "people waiting at the front gate when I leave for my walk and others there when I return." Much remains unchanged today, including the Presbyterian Church where he met his future wife, Bess, and the county courthouse where he began his political career.

The value of such walks, not only in Independence but in one's own treasured places, was captured in Longfellow's words:

> I have an affection for a great city. I feel safe in the neighborhood of man and enjoy the sweet security of the streets.

IOWA CITY

IOWA

On November 20, 2008, Iowa City was named a UNESCO "City of Literature," a recognition previously given to only two other cities—Edinburgh, Scotland, and Melbourne, Australia.

The selection process is "based on an attempt to promote the social, economic and cultural development of cities." Consideration is given to signs that literature, drama and poetry are valued within the city, visible presence of libraries and bookstores, literary events, and focus on domestic and foreign literature.

The list of cities has slowly grown, but by 2015 included only some 20 cities, with Iowa City the only "City of Literature" from the U.S. Additions include Dublin, Ireland; Heidelberg, Germany; Barcelona, Spain; Montevideo, Uruguay; and Nottingham, England.

For Iowa City to be named a "City of Literature" is, to a large extent, a recognition of the kind of city it has always been.

It began in 1839 as a result of an act of the Legislative Assembly of the Iowa Territory, due to a desire to locate a capital nearby.

When the state of Iowa was officially admitted to the Union on December 28, 1846, it was only 59 days later, February 25, 1847, that the University of Iowa was founded in the new state capital city.

In 1857, the state capital was moved to Des Moines and for all the years since, the Old Capitol Building has been the heart of the university campus. And the university soon began to lead in the areas of literature and creativity. It is believed to be the first in the world to accept work in theatre, writing, music and art on an equal basis with academic research.

The Iowa Writer's Workshop was established in 1936, and has produced 13 Pulitzer Prize winners. Notable alumni of the University of Iowa have included playwright Tennessee Williams and novelists Flannery O'Conner and John Irving.

In 1967, an International Writing Program was developed and has since hosted over 1400 writers from more than 140 countries.

And the "City of Literature" identity continued to grow. In 1971, the Iowa Playwright's Workshop was begun. In 1976, a Non-Fiction Writing Program was introduced. In 1987, the Iowa Summer Writing Festival began to welcome writers "from 18 to 98."

In 2009, the year following the official "City of Literature" announcement, the Iowa City Book Festival began, featuring readings from prominent authors and other events with a literature theme. The festival, a great time for visitors, typically occurs during a week in October, with as many as 60 events and 100 presenters.

The city and its citizens found a creative way to celebrate their identity while entering the 21st century. In conjunction with a Streetscape Improvement Project in 2000, the Iowa City

Public Art Advisory Committee envisioned a "Literary Walk" celebrating 49 writers, all of whom have ties to Iowa. Along the sidewalks on both sides of Iowa Avenue, bronze plaques have been set into the concrete, containing the writers' names and quotations from their works.

Looking back through history, it's difficult to separate what the university has done from what the city has done, which is probably a further reason for the success—the impressive, virtually seamless working relationship between the two.

For every visitor to Iowa City, the following invitation is extended:

> As you walk along, make sure you pause to read the writers' words, and as you do, imagine their presence where you stand. Many of them once took the exact steps you take, on Iowa land in a city where academia meets Midwestern community.

......................⌘......................

> There is a certain embarrassment about being a storyteller
> in these times when stories are considered not quite as
> satisfying as statements and statements not quite as satisfying
> as statistics; but in the long run a people is known not by its
> statements or its statistics, but by the stories it tells.
> —Flannery O'Connor
> Master of Arts Degree, 1947
> University of Iowa

LINDSBORG

KANSAS

In the middle of Kansas, since 1941, October of odd-numbered years is the traditional time for Svensk Hyllningsfest, a community festival honoring the Swedish immigrant pioneers whose settlement was incorporated in 1879. The official name of the town is Lindsborg, but it is known to many as "Little Sweden."

Although only about 30 percent of the population are Swedish descendants, the Swedish history of the place provides much to celebrate.

One such celebration included the king of Sweden who, as a part of his bicentennial tour in 1976, came to Lindsborg and rededicated the Swedish Pavilion, which had originally been built for the 1904 St. Louis World's Fair, but was relocated in Lindsborg to the benefit of both Bethany College and the community of Lindsborg. The pavilion is now a part of the Old Mill Museum and is listed on the National Historic Register.

Another tradition gained high visibility at the 1939 New York World's Fair, when the Dala horse continued its transformation from a children's toy to a symbolic artifact of Sweden.

For more than 400 years the stocky, carved and painted wooden icon has been a favorite memento, and is a familiar Lindsborg sight, prominently positioned around town.

Another international visitor of some world prominence has left a lasting impact on Lindsborg. When seven-time world chess champion Anatoly Karpov was looking for a quiet place to train for a major New York match, he found both a prairie peacefulness plus an emerging love of chess among both adults and youth. The community ambience was so accepting that it resulted in the founding of Karpov's International School of Chess and an ongoing social chess night every Thursday.

Also adding to this "small-town/world-view" culture is the Birger Sandzén Memorial Gallery. A Swedish-born painter, Sandzén was an art professor at Bethany College, whose work featured landscape arts and watercolors of the American West. Sandzén, considered by some as the "American Van Gogh," passed away in 1954, having arrived in Lindsborg in 1894 and staying for 60 years. Three years later the gallery was opened by his grateful fellow citizens for the purpose of "sharing the arts with the world through the life and vision of Birger Sandzén,"—longtime honored citizen of "Little Sweden."

PADUCAH

KENTUCKY

An old street marker carries the headline, "$5 Bought Paducah," then follows a one-sentence explanation: "In 1827, Gen. Wm. Clark purchased 37,000 acres of land, including the site on which Paducah now stands, for $5."

Some 20 years after launching the 1804 history-making adventure of the Louis & Clark expedition, Clark laid out his plans for a city. In a letter to his son, dated April 27, 1827, Clark wrote, "I expect to go to the mouth of the Tennessee River, and be absent about two weeks. I have laid out a town there and intend to sell some lots in it, the name is Paducah."

The location, the confluence of the Ohio and Tennessee Rivers, proved generally beneficial to the growth of the town for more than 100 years, until heavy rainfall caused the rivers to flood, cresting at 60.8 feet, and the city was evacuated.

Today, downtown Paducah still carries reminders of the damage. On some of the oldest buildings are the flood's high-water marks, but there also are the Floodwall Murals, a fortification against any recurrence, containing more than 50 murals; for the residents it is "Wall to Wall, Portraits of Our

Past." It's also a confluence of two important Paducah themes: art and the river.

In 2013, the United Nations Education, Scientific and Cultural Organization (UNESCO) named Paducah the world's seventh City of Crafts and Folk Art, for its important role in connectivity of cultures through creativity.

Among other evidences of the appropriateness of this UNESCO distinction is the National Quilt Museum of the United States, where 40,000 visitors per year marvel at the creative artistry displayed from the 500 quilts in the permanent collection and the additional rotating exhibits. The quilts, and the visitors, come from around the world.

Not far from the new Quilt Museum's artfully designed modern facility are several streets filled with older buildings, many retaining the evidence of historical and architectural significance. A conceptual paper on one of those grand buildings, the 1927 Columbia Theatre, reflected on the retained value to community that such buildings continue to possess in Paducah, and all our cities:

> Theatres such as the Columbia speak to the spirit of place, helping tell the unique story of Paducah and its inhabitants. Generations of patrons hold these cherished memories close to their hearts and are willing to make great efforts to assure that the physical touchstone to these memories, the theatre itself, is not lost.

ROCHESTER

MINNESOTA

In 1854, the Western Stage Company, operating out of Dubuque, Iowa, established a stagecoach route to St. Paul, Minnesota. The stagecoaches averaged 40 miles per day in the summer and 25 miles in the winter, while traveling 15 hours per day, so overnight stops were necessary for the maximum of 14 passengers and driver. Rochester emerged as an appropriate stagecoach stop on the route. Within six years, its population had grown to 1,400.

As transportation improved, the railroad soon followed and by 1880, Rochester was becoming a regional market center with a population of more than 5,000.

One of the recent residents was a physician named William Worrall Mayo, who arrived in Rochester in 1863 to become an examining surgeon of federal draftees during the Civil War. He then stayed in Rochester and became the "County Doctor."

On August 12, 1883, a violent tornado struck Rochester, killing 24 people, injuring 100 more and destroying 150 buildings. Dr. Mayo and the Sisters of Saint Francis worked together to address the needs of the many who were injured. The need for a way to provide ongoing health care in the area resulted in the opening, in 1889, of St. Mary's Hospital, including 27 beds.

And as the history of Rochester is recorded, these efforts, originating in response to a terrible tornado, "would set in motion the development of what has become one of the world's foremost centers of medical care."

By 1929, there were 386 physicians in Rochester working with William and Charles, Mayo's sons. Facilities were expanding as well and in 1966, older hospitals were replaced with a new 794-bed Rochester Methodist Hospital.

In 2016, the Mayo Clinic employed more than 4,500 physicians and scientists and 57,100 allied health staff. More than 1.3 million patients from all 50 states and more than 150 countries are seen each year.

A visit to Rochester provides personal insight into the mutually rewarding relationship between the city and the Mayo Clinic that has spanned more than 120 years.

The history has been well preserved in places such as Mayowood Mansion, the Plummer House and the Plummer Building.

Mayowood Mansion was owned by the Olmstead County Historical Society, which maintained the estate as it was when last occupied by Dr. and Mrs. Charles Mayo until 1939 and "is used to interpret the lives of this famous medical family." In 2013 the title was transferred to Mayo Clinic.

The Plummer House was the home of Dr. Henry Plummer and his wife, Daisy. Plummer, who is considered one of the early co-founders of Mayo Clinic, was a renaissance man whose interests included, in addition to medicine, the arts, engineering and architecture (the house today continues to reflect many of his interests). Dr. Mayo said that hiring Dr. Plummer was "the best day's work he ever did."

The Plummer Building in downtown Rochester adds a distinctive touch to the skyline of the city and the 56-bell carillon, mounted in the tower, fills the downtown with periodic "gifts of music."

Music also is a regular feature at Mayo Clinic Hospital. In St. Mary's Chapel, Sunday afternoon organ concerts are a regular occurrence. Mayo Clinic explains, "Among the hospital's most remarkable instruments is the organ in Saint Mary's Chapel, which evokes the prayer of St. Francis of Assisi, 'Lord, make me an instrument of Thy peace.'" As Dr. Will Mayo said, "There is a spiritual as well as a material quality to the care of sick people." The organ was installed in 1932.

Rochester is frequently listed near the top of America's best places to live, and the future is filled with optimism. In an October 2016 article, *Livability's* Matt Carmichael wrote:

> . . . the famed Mayo Clinic medical campus is set to expand big-time. In the next 20 years, fueled by $6 billion in development from public and private sources, Mayo will build the "Destination Medical Center" here. That could lead to 40,000 new jobs and as many as 100,000 new residents according to Mayor Ardell Brede. Brede thinks the city can and will be ready for it. "I think 98 per cent of the cities in the U.S. would love to have this challenge," he says.

Later in the article, Carmichael wrote, "This is how an institution can change a city."

SPRINGFIELD

ILLINOIS

The first settlers were trappers and traders along the Sangamon River in 1818. The first name of the settlement was Calhoun, after Sen. John C. Calhoun of South Carolina. Then, in 1832, the name was changed to Springfield, after a very prosperous Springfield, Massachusetts. But the name most associated with the city's history is in its motto: "Home of President Abraham Lincoln."

Lincoln lived in Springfield for 24 years (1837-61) and his house, which is still there, was the only home he ever owned. He purchased the house in 1944 as the place where he and his wife, Mary Todd, lived and raised their four sons. Today, the National Park Service preserves it in keeping with the Lincoln years for the benefit of a steady flow of visitors.

On February 11, 1861, the newly elected president bid farewell to his hometown when he said, "To this place, and the kindness of these people, I owe everything. Here I have lived a quarter of a century, and have passed from a young to an old man. Here my children have been born, and one is buried. I now leave, not knowing when or whether ever I may return. . . ."

Following his assassination, his body was returned to Springfield. Oak Ridge Cemetery, location of the Lincoln Tomb, is the second most visited cemetery in the U.S. after Arlington National Cemetery.

And when the Lincoln Presidential Library complex opened in 2005, it was received enthusiastically. Within less than two years, crowds had exceeded one million.

In addition to the Lincoln House, there are two other rather historical houses of note in Springfield. The Dana-Thomas House is considered one of the best examples of Frank Lloyd Wright's "Prairie period." With 35 rooms in 12,000 square feet, it provides evidence for the reason the American Institute of Architects named Wright "the greatest American architect of all time."

The Vachel Lindsay Home, site of both his birth and death, has been restored to honor the poetry and the memory of the American poet. Lindsay was born in Springfield in 1879, less than 20 years after Lincoln's death. His poem, "Abraham Lincoln Walks at Midnight," expresses the awareness of his continuing presence, opening with the lines:

> It is portentous, and a thing of state
> That here at midnight, in our little town
> A mourning figure walks, and will not rest.
> Near the old court-house pacing up and down.

And later:

> He is among us:—as in times before!

STURGIS

SOUTH DAKOTA

Since 1938, why have motorcycle riders descended on Sturgis, South Dakota (population 6,627), exceeding 700,000 bikers in 2015? And how did this massive annual bike rally get started? Would you believe the invention of the refrigerator was the genesis?

J.C "Pappy" Hoel, a resident of Sturgis, saw his ice business dying in the early 1930s as sales of refrigerators became a household necessity. Infatuated with motorcycles, in 1936 he purchased an Indian motorcycle franchise with the hope of building the one and only company of its kind in Sturgis. Unfortunately, the Depression of the 1930s was not an auspicious time for new businesses. To create and build interest in motorcycles, he formed the Jackpine Gypsies Motorcycle Club, which in 1938 hosted a dirt track race with nine riders and 800 attendees. That was the start of the annual summer pilgrimage to Sturgis for serious and weekend bikers alike, and has defined it as "Motorcycle City, USA." Sturgis is to motorcycles what Kleenex is to tissues.

For non-bikers, the Sturgis Motorcycle Rally may be an overwhelming experience, but it is surely a unique American "extravaganza," one that can be enjoyed "using kid-friendly caution." At non-rally times, the Sturgis Motorcycle Museum and Hall of Fame provides an opportunity to experience the event without the crush of half a million roaring bikes. At the same time, this is a community with a rich mining history and the incomparable geography surrounding Sturgis.

The natural geography of Custer State Park, Badlands National Park, the Spearfish Canyon Scenic Byways and Devil's Tower National Monument showcase the natural protected beauty of the area, while Mt. Rushmore National Memorial and the Crazy Horse Memorial reflect the creative genius memorializing American greats in dramatic carved rock faces.

......................⌒⟋......................

In some ways, cities and motorcycles share much in common.

When Tom Peters and Bob Waterman wrote their widely popular book, *In Search of Excellence,* the topic of motorcycles found its way into the book. They wrote:

. . . so much of excellence in performance has to do with people's being motivated by compelling . . . values. As Robert Pirsig laments in *Zen and the Art of Motorcycle Maintenance:*

> *While at work I was thinking about this lack of care in the digital computer manuals. . . . Implicit in every line is the idea that 'Here is the machine, isolated in time and space from everything else in the universe. . . .' We were all spectators. It then occurred to me there is no manual that deals with the real business of motorcycle maintenance, the most important aspect of all. Caring about what you're doing is considered either unimportant or taken for granted.*

CREATING A SENSE OF PLACE

GARY MCCALEB

Ultimately, the leaders of cities must reckon with the reality that the places where people enjoy living must be more than steel, asphalt and concrete.

An intangible component plays an important role in creating what is sometimes called "a sense of place." And sometimes there are ways that a small-to-midsize city can be just the right size to create that special sense.

Luke Barr captures that special quality in a well-written piece about Aix-en-Provence (population 141,000) in the south of France.

But his words describe the kind of place most people would love to call "home" anywhere in the world.

Barr writes:

> . . . the town pulls you toward its heart, its grand central street, the Cours Mirabeau. With two tall rows of plane trees and a series of fountains and cafés, it makes you slow down and exhale. M.F. [celebrated writer, M.F.K. Fisher] described the Cours this way: "It is a man-made miracle, perhaps indescribable, compounded of stone

and water and trees, and to the fortunate it is one of the world's chosen spots for their own sentient growth."

Barr ate dinner at the famous café on the Cours, Les Deux Garcons, "never a place one came for the food, but rather for the ambience"—a place built in 1792 which counted among its guests Cézanne, Zola and Hemingway.

But for a place to really be "home" requires more than a walkable, friendly, tree-lined main street and a popular café—and Barr revealed there is more.

There was "a routine, a rhythm, a kind of easygoing daily schedule. . . . The main event was the farmers' market in downtown Aix. On the Place Richelme, under the shade of a canopy of tall plane trees, this was a farmers' market to end all farmers' markets. Not that it was very big, or particularly fancy, but it was idyllic; the market was busy from early morning until just after lunch . . . . "

There also are the inanimate landmarks that somehow acquire an endearing personality. For Barr it was "the fountain of the Four Dolphins . . . our family favorite . . . the fountain consisted of four stone dolphins, smiling and cheerful but each with a slightly different expression, spouting thin streams of water . . . ."

Barr's father remembered the fountain from when he was 13, and "here it was, 50 years later, and still wonderful."

A street, a café, a market, a fountain—together they transcended the generic uses of asphalt and concrete to create a sense of place.

Based on the 2000 Census there were slightly more than 3,300 five-figure cities in the U.S.—and thousands more throughout the world (see note below).

So what would it take for one of those places to emerge so clearly from the others?

Orvieto, Italy, was described by Maureen B. Fant as a "perfect small town." She elaborates, ". . . I cannot find a thing wrong with the medieval center of Orvieto, where some 23,000 souls live atop a tufa outcropping."

Located about an hour's train ride from Rome, Orvieto claims two "perfect streets for strolling and shopping"—Via del Duomo and Corso Cavour.

Other factors in the composition of this "perfection" include: a funicular for transportation, the Gothic Duomo with "world-class frescoes and sculpture," an "excellent, recently renovated archaeological museum" and "gastronomic thrills" provided by Orvietani cooks.

In summary, Orvieto: small, beautiful, perfect.

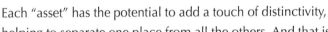

Each "asset" has the potential to add a touch of distinctivity, helping to separate one place from all the others. And that is a challenge when considering the vast number of places in the United States.

Based on the 2000 census, there were approximately:

  9   seven-figure cities with population totaling approximately 23 million

240   six-figure cities with population totaling approximately 54 million

3,300   five-figure cities with population totaling approximately 90.3 million

10,750   four-figure cities with population totaling approximately 37 million

9,700   three-figure cities with population totaling approximately 4.4 million

Therefore, of the 208.7 million Americans living in cities with population of at least 100:

11%   live in seven-figure cities
26%   live in six-figure cities
43%   live in five-figure cities
18%   live in four-figure cities
2%   live in three-figure cities

Joel Kotkin, in an article titled "There's No Place Like Home," pointed out that with so many small towns, "the average local jurisdiction population in the United States is 6,200, small enough to allow nonprofessional politicians to have a serious impact."

TREASURED PLACES
OF THE
WEST

ASHLAND

OREGON

Ashland, Oregon, population 20,000, may very well be the home of the largest not-for-profit theater in the U.S. And it's a rather impressive, and instructive, story.

The story begins in 1893 when the people of Ashland constructed a Chautauqua building, as part of a phenomenon that began in 1874 on the shores of Lake Chautauqua in the state of New York and spread across the nation, bringing education and entertainment to dispersed and sometimes isolated towns of the pre-radio era. Theodore Roosevelt called the Chautauqua "the most American thing in America."

By 1905, the Chautauqua building in Ashland was enlarged to accommodate 1,500. Performers included John Philip Sousa and William Jennings Bryan. But some 20 years later, the audiences began to decline as radio and movies became more available.

The building began to deteriorate, to the extent that in the early 1930s, the dome and parts of the building were torn down. But the cement walls were still standing.

Such circumstances are often the beginning of the last sad chapter of a story.

But not this time. Instead, it was the beginning of a new and exciting sequel. And an illustration of the potential impact of one person's idea when it is given the chance to live.

As Angus Bowmer viewed the old, abandoned cement walls of the Chautauqua building, he was strangely reminded of sketches he had seen of Elizabethan theaters. And so this proud, visionary citizen of Ashland proposed a way to celebrate the Fourth of July in 1935 with a Shakespearian celebration. He received an encouraging advance from the city of a sum "not to exceed $400" to launch his project.

An optimistic, yet prophetic flyer was circulated announcing the "First Annual Shakespeare Festival." Reserved seats were $1, general admission 50 cents and children 25 cents. The performance on July 2 was *Twelfth Night*, *The Merchant of Venice* was presented on July 3 and *Twelfth Night* was repeated on July 4. Ticket sales were sufficient to cover expenses.

In retrospect, it was a small, but successful beginning.

In 2010, Ashland celebrated the 75th anniversary of what is now known as the Oregon Shakespeare Festival with a record attendance of 414,783 for a season that now runs from February to October, presenting 11 plays in three theaters. Over the intervening years, each one of Shakespeare's 37 plays have been staged at least three times.

A few highlights from the Oregon Shakespeare Festival timeline include:

- 30-minute adaptations were broadcast by NBC radio from 1951-74
- a second theater was added in 1970 and a third in 1977

- the festival won a Tony Award in 1983 for outstanding achievement in regional theater
- In 2001 the 10 millionth ticketholder was celebrated

Today, supported by hundreds of volunteers, employing about 500 people, and visited by a national and international audience, the Oregon Shakespeare Festival has a major economic and cultural impact on the city and surrounding region.

And the "Chautauqua walls remain standing; covered with ivy, they surround the Allen Elizabethan Theatre . . . and serve as a reminder of the immense determination, commitment and innovation of all who have come before."

How far that little candle throws his beams!
—Shakespeare
Merchant of Venice

ASTORIA

OREGON

On November 15, 1805, at the last campsite before arriving at the Pacific, Capt. William Clark wrote in his journal, "About 3 o'clock the wind lulled, and the River became calm. I had the canoes loaded in great haste and set out from this dismal nitch where we had been confined for 6 days passed, without the possibility of proceeding on, returning to a better situation, or get out to hunt. Scarce provisions, and torents [sic] of rain poreing on us all the time."

For years, on Washington State Route 401 across the Columbia River just outside Astoria, Oregon, travelers have frequented the Dismal Nitch Rest Stop located in the area where Lewis and Clark made their last campsite before completing their journey to the Pacific Ocean.

And just south of Astoria is Fort Clatsop, the replica marking the place where the group stayed from November to March, establishing American presence with the posting of the American flag. The fort and surrounding historic trails are all part of the Lewis and Clark National Historical Park.

A few miles further south along the scenic Pacific coast is Seaside, where we found walkability a natural feature of the community. A one-and-a-half mile Seaside Promenade runs along the coastline and somewhere near mid-point intersects with the Turnaround, leading through the highly busy traffic of both pedestrians and autos. A perfectly located huge bronze statue of Lewis and Clark, with their dog, Seaman, looking out across the Pacific horizon, celebrates the history of the places to all who pass by.

Continuing south on the Promenade is the location of the Salt Cairn, or Salt Works, where, according to their records, by February 1806 some of the men of the Lewis and Clark Party, boiling kettles of ocean water 24 hours a day, had produced 28 gallons of "excellent, fine, strong & white" salt to preserve meat in preparation for the return journey.

Five years later, in 1811, John Jacob Astor based his American Fur Company near the mouth of the beautiful Columbia River and founded Fort Astoria, the first permanent settlement on the Pacific coast.

The fishing industry was a strong economic base for Astoria through most of the 20th century. Today, a walk along the Waterfront Trail leads from the pier, through downtown, passing along the old canneries and new restaurants. Residents value their history and view the older structures as one of their greatest assets. Tourism is becoming an increasingly important economic factor.

Astoria is the oldest American settlement west of the Rocky Mountains. Thousands visit each year, still coming by way of the water, but in cruise ships rather than canoes. There were 33 people in the Lewis and Clark expedition party, today the annual estimate of cruise ship visitors approaches 50,000.

Many climb the 164-step spiral staircase of the Astoria Column, built in 1926, and view the grand expanse that Lewis and Clark witnessed more than 200 years ago.

Reflecting on the vivid scene of the sidewalks of Seaside:

> In real life, only from the ordinary adults of the city sidewalks do children learn—if they learn at all—the first fundamental of successful city life. People must take a modicum of public responsibility for each other even if they have no ties to each other. This is a lesson nobody learns by being told. It is learned from the experience of having other people without ties of kinship or close friendship or formal responsibility take a modicum of public responsibility for you.
>
> —Jane Jacobs
> *The Death and Life of Great American Cities*

BILLINGS

MONTANA

The skyline is the first indication that Billings is not just another typical American city. A dramatic backdrop rising hundreds of feet above the valley floor surrounds the northern and eastern edge of the city, enhanced by the rising and setting of the sun.

Billings is a city that has mastered the art of maximizing its relationship with its surroundings.

Named for Frederick Billings, the former president of Northern Pacific Railroad, in recognition of its birth as a railroad stop in 1882, Billings balances the natural beauty of the Rimrocks on the north with the free-flowing Yellowstone River on the south. And driving southwest from Billings, a traveler will enjoy the Beartooth Highway, which Charles Kuralt dubbed "the most beautiful drive in America." It has been labeled an "All-American Road," meeting such standards as possessing intrinsic features that do not exist elsewhere, "important enough to be tourist designations into themselves."

Five miles southwest of Billings is the Pictograph Cave, a National Historic Landmark containing more than 100 ancient rock paintings.

And 28 miles east of Billings is a rock location with singular historic significance: Pompeys Pillar National Monument. In 1806, William Clark passed through the area and wrote in his journal: "At 4 pm arrived at a remarkable rock. . . . this rock I ascended and from it's [sic] top had a most extensive view in every direction." Clark carved into the rock: "W Clark July 25, 1806." It is the only remaining visible physical evidence of the Lewis and Clark expedition. He named the place Pompeys Pillar after the son of his Lemhi Shoshone guide, Sacajawea.

In the winter, Billings is the "Trailhead to Montana Winter Adventure"—another opportunity to cast the city's role as a nice combination of the indoor adventure (Moss Mansion, Yellowstone Art Museum and Western Heritage Center) with the outdoor (cross country skiing, ice climbing, dog sledding and snowmobiling).

After all, this is the state about which John Steinbeck wrote, "I'm in love with Montana, for other states I have admiration, respect, recognition, even some affection. But with Montana it is love. And it's difficult to analyze love when you're in it."

.... ⌒ ....

The importance of maximizing the relationship of a city with its surroundings has multiple implications. In another Montana city, Daniel Kemmis, the former mayor of Missoula, speaks from experience in his book, *The Good City and the Good Life*.

> By referring time and again to imaginary places called, in our political discourse, "rural America," "urban America," and "suburban America," we create an image and a practice of separate urban, rural, and suburban polities, and we all but eliminate the possibility of acting upon a sound understanding of how city center, suburbs, and rural surroundings might together operate as an effective engine of economic prosperity.

BOULDER CITY

NEVADA

"The Boulder Canyon Project (construction of the Hoover Dam) was the most significant American public works project of the 20th century." It was and remains a model for federal government vision and leadership and private sector collaboration. To this day, the sight of this majestic dam continues to challenge and excite the imagination as an engineering wonder and iconic personification of America at its best.

Completed in 1935, the middle of the depression, Boulder Dam Project was designed to control flooding and land reclamation, provide water and power for the growing population of southern California as well as water for the agricultural valleys of the west. At a time of unprecedented unemployment, it provided jobs for more than 4,000 workers and created a need and opportunity to build a city to house the employees and their families.

In fact, Boulder City is itself as remarkable as the construction of the dam. It was "conceived by the Federal Government as an ideal town, a 'model' city, to which the American people could look for hope of a better future." And it "holds national importance for its place in the history of American city planning" by introducing design concepts that were both "innovative and experimental, separating residential and business streets from through-streets, dividing city functions into specific business, residential and industrial zones; making the government center a community focal point; and establishing a greenbelt to buffer the town from the dessert."

Equally important was a commitment to addressing quality of life issues, including parks, recreation, schools, and public safety and an appreciation of the importance of effective management and financial structures and local government systems. Created to serve the thousands of workers employed by the Boulder Canyon Project, Boulder City has evolved and benefited from the original concepts and plans, enriched by its history but not constrained by its past.

In many ways Boulder City could be a small New England town with a western feel, not a replica or offshoot of nearby Las Vegas. There are no casinos in the city limits. And while the town itself and the recreational opportunities in the area are attractions, Hoover Dam clearly is what draws thousands of tourists to experience this man-made wonder.

A movie, museum and guided tour provide an engaging history of the building of the dam, both the positive as well as the worst elements of our history, e.g. explicit discrimination against African Americans and Asian Americans and limited commitment to the safety of employees.

It is a challenge to the imagination to realize that construction of the dam required the building of a railroad, the creation of a concrete manufacturing plant and a fabricating facility to build the massive hydro-electric power turbines in the middle of a desert.

With the dam as an economic engine for the economy, both as a significant generator of hydro-electric power and a tourist attraction, Boulder City has an appeal for those interested in the history of city design, the commitment to balancing development and respecting the environment, as well as activities that are just plain fun. There are bike and hiking trails, zip-line challenges at 50 miles per hour, multiple golf courses, a railroad museum, and airplane tours.

Hoover Dam and the city it spawned reflect the vision, creativity and success of federal leadership at its best.

CARMEL-BY-THE-SEA

CALIFORNIA

When *Condé Nast Traveler* magazine published the results of its 2009 readers' choice awards for the Top Cities in the World, the section was introduced by a quote from Aristotle:

> A great city is not to be confounded with a populous one.

Following, on the same page, was a list of the 50 top cities in the world. Those from the U.S. included San Francisco and New York City, among others. And there on the list with Chicago above and Boston below was Carmel with a special notation, which read:

"The smallest of all 50 cities listed here has 3,894 citizens—and two million annual visitors."

It was in 1602 that Spanish explorer and Carmelite friar Sebastian Vizcaino discovered this little valley and named it for his patron saint, Our Lady of Mt. Carmel.

After the 1906 San Francisco earthquake, an artist colony developed as painters, musicians and writers took advantage of an appealing offer from Carmel to acquire a home lot for $10 down, little or no interest and whatever they could pay on a monthly basis. Jack London wrote about this artist colony in his novel *The Valley of the Moon*.

Checking Carmel's website, it seems this very small-great city is indeed something of a paradox—and likes it that way. For example: "This is a place to get away from it all without sacrificing the big-city offerings of art, theater, music, and dining."

The approach to a city plan is apparently intentionally casual: "The walkable warren of streets whose slope is dictated by trees, houses unnumbered, storefronts and cottages, harkening back to a time when everybody knew everybody else by name. It is, in large part, still like that. In lieu of street numbers, cottages bear names as quirky as racehorses'."

Carmel's appeal is multifaceted—it's known as an artists' colony and a jewel city—and its reputation for being among the most pet-friendly cities has grown to the point it has been called "DogTown." And when Carmel resident Clint Eastwood announced his candidacy for mayor, *People* magazine's story carried the headline, "Promising a New Spirit—and Freedom of Ice Cream—Clint Eastwood Tackles his Toughest Role: Mayoral Candidate." Eastwood won the election and a two-year mayoral term in 1986 and local ordinances were made less restrictive.

But among all its credits, walkability reigns supreme—as they say in Carmel, "Best of all, you can always walk home."

Or you could elect to take the 17-Mile Drive—"An old horse trail that meandered south to Carmel" (from the Del Monte Hotel, built in 1880). The round trip totaled 17 miles. It is a trip of history and beauty intertwined, and it was experienced anew in Mark Frost's bestseller *The Match*:

> The rituals and revels of the Clambake began, as they did every year, on Tuesday night . . . and for the next seven days this hamlet by the sea transformed into the center of high society in North America. . . . Most of the PGA Tour players are bunked at the old Pine Inn in Carmel or at a hotel in Monterey called Casa Munras. At dozens of parties up and down the Seventeen-Mile Drive, on that Tuesday evening friendships and rivalries formed or rekindled in anticipation of the coming competition.

> Bing Crosby always hosted a low-key affair at his own house just off the thirteenth green at Pebble Beach. . . .

Pebble Beach Golf Links is rated the #1 Public Golf Course in America and the 17-Mile Drive provides its travelers what has been called "the most sublime collision of land and sea anywhere in the world."

CHEYENNE

WYOMING

On July 10, 1890, President Benjamin Harrison's signature officially made Wyoming the 44th state and Cheyenne was named the capital.

Seven years later, in 1897, an event was organized that has celebrated Cheyenne and its Wyoming heritage to this day. The event was called Cheyenne Frontier Days and has become a well-known story of the inseparable relationship between the community and its citizens:

Having passed its 120th year, the Cheyenne Frontier Days draws some 200,000 people annually, in the 10-day span of the event (always around the last full week of July). In Cheyenne (population 60,000) these are known as "the best 10 days of the year."

The annual "Walking of the Steers" is held on the Sunday morning preceding the event, during which as many as 400 or more steers walk a three-mile course through the streets of Cheyenne. The idea was inspired by the "running of the bulls" in Pamplona, Spain.

To honor the Wyoming heritage, and the Cheyenne Nation, home of one of the most famous tribes of the Great Plains, there is a permanent campground, "Indian Village," which hosts authentic dancing, music, storytelling and food.

The rodeo itself, known as the "Daddy of 'Em All," has repeatedly received the Professional Rodeo Cowboys Association's "Outdoor Rodeo of the Year" award, including 11 consecutive times from 2004 to 2014. The arena seats 19,000.

In 1952 the Cheyenne Frontier Committee served a free pancake breakfast. By 1996 a single- day record was set when 16,897 people were served. All the work is done by volunteers, welcoming the thousands of worldwide visitors with a touch of western hospitality. Annual estimates include 100,000 flapjacks, 3,000 pounds of ham and 520 gallons of coffee being served.

To add even more history to this legendary event, the *Denver Post* reinstated the Frontier Days Train carrying a sold-out group of 700 riders on a one-day round trip to Cheyenne aboard 1950s-era passenger cars pulled by the Union Pacific's vintage steam locomotive No. 844.

The "Bucking Horse and Rider" logo is a registered trademark of the state of Wyoming. You will see it on the Wyoming license plate and the state quarter. The rider is said to honor Clayton Danks, who was a three-time champion in the rodeo, beginning in 1904. The horse, according to legend, is Steamboat, "one of the best bucking horses of all time" and known as "the horse that couldn't be ridden." Steamboat was inducted into the National Cowboy Hall of Fame and was buried in the rodeo grounds near bucking chute No. 9.

The presence of Frontier Days is not limited to 10 days. The Cheyenne Frontier Days Old West Museum is open year-round and tells the intertwined history of the Frontier Days—the city and the celebration. The Cheyenne Frontier Days Hall of Fame is there.

We've been to Cheyenne twice, but unfortunately neither visit was during "the best 10 days of the year" but it seemed to us the spirit of this Cheyenne western hospitality spills over into all the other days of the year. While in the museum we met one of the volunteers, who told us that she and her husband had moved away because of a business opportunity, but they missed being a part of the year-round Frontier volunteers and they "just had to move back to Cheyenne."

Bill Dubois may have captured this feeling when he was inducted into the Cheyenne Frontier Days Hall of Fame after volunteering for more than 40 years. He was one of more than 12,500 volunteers who work throughout the year to welcome next year's massive wave of visitors to the 10-day celebration. When asked why he did it, Dubois replied, "It's the Cheyenne thing to do."

CODY

WYOMING

If you Google *Cody, Wyoming,* you may find this statement:

> Cody, Wyoming, was founded in 1896 by the living
> legend, Colonel William F. 'Buffalo Bill' Cody, who at the
> age of 41 was one of the most famous men in the world.

To a great extent, to visit Cody is to experience the personality of the man, his story and his Wild West.

William Frederick Cody was born in 1846. After his father died, Bill started working at age 11 and at age 14 he was riding for the Pony Express. Later, he worked as a civilian scout for the Army, sometimes also serving as a buffalo hunter to supply meat for the soldiers. It was during his buffalo hunting days that he acquired the nickname Buffalo Bill.

In 1883, Cody started a circus-like show called Buffalo Bill's Wild West, which toured the U.S. and Europe. Queen Victoria attended one of the performances in England.

After he founded his town, he soon opened the Hotel Irma, named for his daughter. Celebrating its 100th anniversary in 2002, the hotel continues to be a popular part of the legend of Buffalo Bill.

And there is no better place to experience a real cowboy rodeo than Cody in the summertime, which is why it's called the "Rodeo Capital of the World." Cody Nite Rodeo is scheduled every night from June 1 through August 31. All the participants are amateurs, riding for their love of cowboy life.

The professionals also come to Cody. The Cody Stampede Rodeo, an official PRCA (Professional Rodeo Cowboys Association) event has been held every year over the Independence Day holiday since 1919.

A visit to Old Trail Town recreates the feelings of walking through the early days of the West. Some 25 historic western buildings, as much as 100 years old, have been restored and are filled with connections to stories of the past, such as Butch Cassidy and the Sundance Kid and the tales of Jeremiah Johnson.

In all of the ways mentioned above, the 9,500 citizens of Cody have done an excellent job of preserving the story of Buffalo Bill's Wild West. But there is so much more.

When the Cody Chamber of Commerce makes the following statement: "Cody is home to one of the country's supreme cultural attractions—the five-museum complex of the Buffalo Bill Center of the West"—one visit is all that's necessary to know that it's not braggin', it's true.

Averaging 175,000 visitors annually, there is something for every age to enjoy within the expansive space of the five museums, which includes the Whitney Gallery of Western Art, the Plains Indian Museum, the Buffalo Bill Museum, the Cody Firearms Museum and the Draper Museum of National History.

The Buffalo Bill Center is a great asset to the town of Cody. But it also is a commentary on the undaunted spirit of the people who live there, represented by more than 300 volunteers who donate more than 14,000 hours annually to the center. They, like the summertime amateur cowboys, are a living continuation "of the spirit of individual accomplishment, western hospitality, honesty and friendliness," and joint cooperation of the citizens as was instilled in the early settlers by the 'Old Scout.'

......................⌒..........................

In every city there is some new thing which waits
to be done with distinction.
—James Michener
The Quality of Life

FRIDAY HARBOR

WASHINGTON

As the story goes, heading into the 1850s there was not a clear understanding as to whether San Juan Island was British or U.S. soil. As a slow trickle of American citizens began to settle there, the Hudson Bay Company established a presence with a salmon-curing station, followed by a sheep ranch. The co-existence was tolerated, with each side assuming they were in the right, until one June day in 1859 when a U.S. settler shot a pig that had wandered into his garden; it was subsequently discovered that the pig was British, belonging to the Hudson Bay Company.

The inability to successfully settle the matter resulted in what one British military officer frustratedly called "two great nations in a war over a squabble about a pig." U.S. presence ultimately counted more than 400 troops and 14 cannons facing off against five British warships loaded with 167 guns.

No shot was ever fired. But San Juan remained under joint military occupation for 12 years.

The dispute was eventually referred to Kaiser Wilhelm I of Germany who ruled in favor of the U.S. in October 1872.

One Hudson Bay Company employee from Hawaii settled on the island, living in a protected harbor while working as a sheepherder. As the story, now legend, continues, his campsite became familiar to the sailors frequenting the harbor area. His name was Joe Friday and soon it became natural for the sailors to refer to the location as "Friday's Harbor," and eventually it was simply Friday Harbor.

On February 10, 1909, Friday Harbor became the only incorporated town in the San Juan Islands. Departing ships were essential to the economy as they carried loads of apples, pears, cherries, strawberries and peas, among other things, to the mainland. In the 1970s, a new kind of economy began to emerge, including retirees, real estate development, construction and tourism.

Only a few steps off the ferry are necessary to be on the streets of Friday Harbor's one-square-mile of walkability, with no stoplights, billboards or chain stores.

A printed copy of the self-guided walking tour will lead a visitor through 26 historic points. The first is Memorial Park, which since 1890 has "been the meeting place for those arriving and departing" Friday Harbor.

Also along the walkable downtown is The Whale Museum, "opened in 1979 as the first museum in the country devoted to a species living in the wild." The museum, combined with unique opportunities for whale watching from land or tour boats, and kayaking, yields an experience in the Pacific Northwest virtually unchanged by the passing of more than the 100 years of the life of Friday Harbor. In the town there is evidence of positive change, but leaving town, passing through the surrounding setting of the San Juan islands, one has the sense that the stories and the scenic beauty have been preserved unchanged.

GRAND CANYON VILLAGE

ARIZONA

Early visitors to Grand Canyon traveled by stagecoach. But beginning in 1901, the Atchison, Topeka and Santa Fe Railroad opened the Grand Canyon Railway and hundreds of visitors have stepped off the train each day, thereby increasing the daily population. This distinctive village of some 2,000 residents broke the 6 million mark for annual visitors in 2016 (which means, very conservatively, some 10,000 new visitors per day enjoy the natural beauty of the surroundings and the genial hospitality of the more permanent residents).

The El Tovar, one of the Fred Harvey railroad hotels, opened in 1905 and continues to provide lodging and dining opportunities overlooking the South Rim.

The work of Mary E.J. Coulter (one of the first female architects and chief architect and designer for the Fred Harvey Company for more than 35 years) includes the Hopi House (1905), in which Colter wanted to honor the history of the people who had inhabited the Grand Canyon area for hundreds of years. The building was designed as a Hopi dwelling. Inside, visitors could watch Hopi jewelry, pottery and blankets being made for sale.

Hermit Rest and Lookout Studio (1914) was designed to appear as though an old hermit piled up nearby stones and available tree limbs to provide an inconspicuous shelter at the canyon rim. As she completed this project, Colter reportedly said, "You can't imagine what it cost to make it look this old."

Later projects included the 70-foot-tall Desert View Watchtower (1932) and Bright Angel Lodge (1935). The "Mary Jane Coulter Buildings" are listed as a National Historic Landmark and every day thousands of visitors witness the artistry of her philosophy as described by Virginia Grattan in her book, *Mary Colter, Builder Upon the Red Earth*:

> Colter's philosophy was that a building should grow out of its setting, embodying the history and flavor of the location. It should belong to its environment as though indigenous to that spot.

The case for designing the built environment to deftly interact with the natural environment is on permanent display in Grand Canyon Village.

Landscape painter Bill Conner's story, carried by BBC on June 15, 2016, told of the years he has spent painting in the Grand Canyon, from which he draws continual inspiration— "You can explore the Grand Canyon your whole life," he said, "and never see it all. It just never ends out here."

A walk between the Coulter buildings, while viewing the changing colors from the setting of the sun on the canyon, adds new meaning to Sophocles' words:

> One must wait until the evening to see
> how splendid the day has been.

HELENA

MONTANA

The year 1864 proved to be very important to the birth and life of this city, which would become the capital of Montana.

In the early 1860s successful gold strikes in Idaho Territory caused the federal government to create, in May 1864, a new territory named Montana. Shortly thereafter, on June 14, 1864, a group of prospectors called the "Four Georgians" discovered gold near Prickly Pear Creek and set up a mining camp called Last Chance Gulch. Today, the main street in downtown Helena is named Last Chance Gulch. A walking tour through the Historic District provides the opportunity to revisit the history of the early years.

Within a few months the population of the camp exceeded 200. As the population grew, so also did the dissatisfaction with the name of the camp, which was rapidly becoming a town. So on October 30, 1864, a group gathered to select a new name. The suggestions included Pumpkinville and Squashtown, no doubt a result of meeting the day before Halloween. Considering the alternatives, Helena was a happy choice.

The Montana gold rush continued, with more than $3 billion in gold discovered within the city limits of Helena over a span of 20 years.

Upon arrival in Helena, visitors will quickly notice a highly visible and beautiful landmark, the Cathedral of St. Helena, its design inspired by the Votive Church in Vienna, Austria, and its twin spires soaring 230 feet above the ground. Adorning the top of each spire is a 12-foot-tall cross, gilded appropriately, in gold leaf.

In July 1864, Congress approved the charter for the Northern Pacific Railway to run across the northwestern states from Minnesota to the Pacific. The golden spike signaling the track completion was driven by former President Ulysses Grant some 40 miles west of Helena.

Areas once considered remote were much more connected. One of those connections was with Vaudeville performers and other entertainers who made stops between Chicago and Seattle. Since those early years, citizens of Helena have found ways to combine efforts, bringing a steady stream of arts and entertainment to the area. The most recent iteration is named the Myrna Loy Center in honor of "Montana's First Lady of Film" and former resident of Helena. Loy is perhaps best remembered by the Academy Award nominee *The Thin Man*, but her career included some 125 films. The Myrna Loy Center screens films daily, hosts live performances and an art gallery. In keeping with the spirit of historic preservation, it is housed in the old Lewis and Clark County Jail.

In that same year of 1864, some 1,500 miles from Helena, in St. Louis, on March 19, Charles Marion Russell was born. As a boy he developed a fascination with the open and adventurous Wild West and the stories he heard of prospectors, explorers and fur traders. By the age of 16, he could wait no longer. He left school and headed to Montana, first work-ing on a sheep ranch, then with a hunter-trapper-rancher. He lived with Native Americans for a year, then back to the open spaces, before settling in the area of Great Falls while spending increasing amounts of time as an artist.

Russell lived in Montana for the rest of his life, producing an estimated 4,000 works of art. He was selected to represent the state of Montana in the National Statuary Hall Collection in the U.S. Capitol.

To enjoy the expansiveness of Russell's work, visit the Montana Museum in Helena, which has a collection of more than 200 pieces of his art.

Today, the birth year of the artist and the Montana state capitol are symbolically celebrated together. In the chamber of the House of Representatives is located the most significant piece of capitol art, a 1912 painting by Charles Russell titled "Lewis and Clark Meeting the Flathead Indians at Ross' Hole." The painting is 25 feet long and 12 feet high and was com-missioned by the state of Montana to commemorate a day in history—September 4, 1805, near Ross' Hole and the east fork of the Bitterroot River, as the Lewis and Clark expedition was crossing southwestern Montana heading westward. But the painting also serves as a reciprocal tribute—artist to his state, state to her artist.

It's a long and close relationship as a book title suggests in referring to him as "Montana's Charlie Russell"—but Russell's reach is longer and wider. Kirby Lambert of the Montana Historical Society has said, "Russell defines the way we think about the West before we had photographs."

JUNEAU

ALASKA

In 1880, Joe Juneau and fellow prospector Richard Harris discovered gold nuggets "as large as peas and beans" near Snow Slide Gulch at the head of Gold Creek. Shortly thereafter, a camp sprang up and in December 1881 a meeting of 72 miners voted to name the settlement Juneau, the first to be founded after Alaska was purchased by the U.S. from Russia in 1867.

From that small and seemingly insignificant beginning, Juneau earned distinction as an "island city," unreachable by roads, only by air or water, yet claiming an area of 3,255 square miles within its city limits, which is larger than the states of Rhode Island or Delaware.

Juneau also can claim the presence of glaciers within its city limits, with some reachable by the local road system. The Mendenhall Glacier, considered the only "urban glacier," is about 10 miles from the downtown area.

In 1900, when the gold rush was flourishing, Juneau was named the capital city of the territory, replacing Sitka. Today, a new industry is flourishing—cruise ship tourism—increasing in numbers and size of ships, and bringing an estimated one million visitors to this city each year.

Disembarking the ship, an opportunity for an entirely different type of ride is nearby. The Mount Roberts Tramway takes some 200,000 annual riders 1,800 feet above Juneau for an expansive view of the surrounding beauty. A small theater located at this tree-line location screens an informative film about the Tlingit culture.

The Tlingit, along with people from the Haida and Tsimshian cultures, gather in Juneau every other year in June for Celebration, a four-day festival filling the city with some 5,000 people, including more than 2,000 dancers.

In *National Geographic Traveler*, May/June 2006, Everett Potter described Juneau in this way:

> It's an arresting image: Hemmed in by the Tongass National Forest and snowcapped mountains, with the mile-and-a-half-wide, ten-story-tall Mendenhall Glacier at its back door, this fiercely independent enclave of 31,000 is arguably the most dramatically sited capital in the United States.

······················ ⚬⁄ ······················

In 1980 the first Sealaska Elders Conference, composed of clan leaders, traditional scholars and elders, founded Sealaska Heritage Institute with the purpose of perpetuating and enhancing Tlingit, Haida and Tsimshian cultures of southeast Alaska and to promote Alaska native arts, cultures, history and education. Special attention is given to reading, math and leadership skills for the children.

The Walter Soboleff Building, dedicated in 2015, is the "traditional bentwood box" to protect the cultural treasures and the aspiration that Juneau becomes the Northwest Coast Art Capital of the World.

KETCHIKAN

ALASKA

When Alaska was purchased by the U.S. in 1867, an area along the southern coast was a popular summer fish camp for the Tlingit people. By 1885, an Irish immigrant had purchased 160 acres from Tlingit Chief Kyan and the town of Ketchikan was established, primarily based upon a fishing economy. And the continual abundance of salmon has given the city a long-term claim on the title "Salmon Capital of the World."

It's an appealing locale for fishermen, but even non-fishing visitors are fascinated by the sight of countless salmon swimming upstream. And this amazing scene can be enjoyed while walking along one of the best boardwalks in the world. The Creek Street Boardwalk is built above the water and surrounded by brightly colored shops and stores.

Reasons for visiting Ketchikan are often neatly summarized in three points:

1. feisty salmon
2. idyllic scenery
3. rich native culture

The "idyllic scenery" features, but is not limited to, the "achingly blue lakes" of Misty Fiords National Monument. Almost anywhere one goes in the very inviting and walkable setting of Ketchikan is worthy of a photograph.

But one of the very most distinctive things about this place is the highly visible signs of a cultural past well preserved, expressed in the silent stories of the standing totem poles—the world's largest collection.

The Totem Heritage Center houses 33 totem poles, the largest acquisitions of unrestored 19th- century specimens, as much as 160 years old, some recovered from deserted settlements.

The "golden age of totem poles" was from the mid-1700s to the late 1800s, a time when the fur trade was flourishing and the Tlingit and other tribes benefitted. Additional money and the availability of iron tools resulted in bigger and better totem poles.

The totem poles served various purposes, but almost all told a story. Some honored important leaders at their death and marked a transition of leadership, in the sense that the next leader was not viewed as fully in charge until a totem pole had been erected as a memorial of the former leader.

Other poles were erected in the front of a house, often displaying the family or clan crest and reflecting the ancestry and social rank of the family, sometimes including geographic origin or family history.

Myths and legends are kept alive in the stories that are told, often including the wildlife of the region. The crow and raven are frequently found in the stories.

The salmon, the scenery and the totem poles have combined to create a successful new economy for Ketchikan—and a new identity.

The "Salmon Capital of the World" is increasingly becoming known as "First City," the first Alaska port of call for northbound ships.

In 2004, Ketchikan's number of visitors per year exceeded 800,000 and has stayed above that number in all succeeding years. There is typically a cruise ship at the dock every day, often more than one, sometimes as many as five.

As the ships approach Ketchikan, the journey for the passengers becomes more than a cruise, it is an adventure, because they have arrived at "the beginning of the last frontier."

MONTEREY

CALIFORNIA

The citizens of Monterey like to think of their hometown as California's "first city." The claim is based, at least partially, on the fact that Monterey had California's first theater, public building, public library, publicly funded school, printing press and newspaper.

But today the first stop for many visitors is the Old Fisherman's Wharf. The wharf has maintained a lively presence in Monterey since its beginning in the 1870s. The popular novels by John Steinbeck—*Cannery Row, Tortilla Flat* and *East of Eden* in the mid-1900s—were all set in the Monterey Bay area. Today, the former Ocean View Avenue, once lined with sardine canneries, carries the name Cannery Row in honor of Steinbeck's book.

The fishing and cannery business began to decline in the 1950s, but the heritage and history of the area, known for its abundance and variety of marine life, was reclaimed when the Monterey Bay Aquarium opened in 1984, locating on the site of a former sardine cannery. Crowds numbering in the range of two million per year continue to flood the aquarium and the old wharf.

And Monterey continues to add to its celebrated distinction of "firsts." The aquarium is the first in the world to grow live California giant kelp. Visitors view from several levels the creatures of the kelp forest in a 28-foot-tall exhibit.

And while it doesn't claim to be first, Monterey does claim the Monterey Jazz Festival to be one of the longest running such festivals in the world, having begun in 1958 and now welcoming an attendance of 200,000 each year.

And there is also a distinctive "last." The only remaining example of a whalebone sidewalk is in front of the 1847 Old Whaling Station, where whale-sighting opportunities are not far away.

Steinbeck once observed that "a great and interesting story is about everyone or it will not last."

Isn't it much the same for a city? That the grand and interesting cities are places where everyone feels included.

In his book *Tortilla Flat*, there is one small example—two sentences—inviting the reader to relate to the story and the citizens, surely, to connect with their city:

> They walked side by side along the dark beach toward Monterey, where the lights hung, necklace above necklace against the hill. The sand dunes crouched along the back of the beach like tired hounds, resting: and the waves gently practiced at striking, and hissed a little.

OGDEN

UTAH

The area including almost all Utah and Nevada, as well as some of the contiguous states, is called the Great Basin. Its first permanent European settlement occurred in 1846, when a trapper named Miles Goodyear established a fort-like trading post at a bend in the Weber River for trappers and travelers.

As the population grew, the name was changed to Ogden, the name of another trapper/explorer and the connection to travelers and traveling has remained.

The story of Ogden is in many ways the story of the railroad. Union Pacific was the first major railroad presence in Utah and within 20 years, it was the largest railroad company in the territory, thanks largely to the development of the Oregon Short Line and Utah Northern Railway.

But May 10, 1869, was the biggest day in Utah's railroad history and an important one in American history: the date of the driving of the golden spike at Promontory Summit, marking the completion of a transcontinental railroad connecting the Central Pacific and the Union Pacific. The rail network was constructed between 1863 and 1869. The 1,085 miles of track connected Sacramento, California, to Council Bluffs, Iowa.

The first transcontinental passengers arrived in California on September 6, 1869. Popularly known as the "Overland Route," it continued in operation until 1962.

The National Park Service has preserved this historic site and receives approximately 45,000 visitors annually. Reenactment ceremonies are regularly held including replica steam locomotives. The golden spike is now in a museum at Stanford University. Engraved on the spike: "May God continue the unity of our country, as the railroad unites the two great oceans of the world."

Since the Union Pacific tracks were laid through Ogden on the way to Promontory Summit, Ogden won the competition with other nearby towns for the "Junction City." A popular motto promoted the east-west, north-south travel opportunities: "You can't get anywhere without coming to Ogden." The first station was built in 1869, but a bigger and much better Union Station, containing 33 hotel rooms and a restaurant, was built in 1889. After a fire destroyed the interior of the station, a new Spanish Colonial Revival-style station was built in 1924 and now serves as the Utah State Railroad Museum. The tag line is "Four Museums, Two Galleries and One Historic Train Station."

While passenger train service was discontinued in May 1997, Ogden continues to welcome travelers, located about 50 miles from Promontory Summit. Visitors to the Sundance Film Festival and winter sports enthusiasts all find reminders of the railroad days in downtown Ogden, especially along the 25th Street approach to Union Station.

The restored Peery's Egyptian Theater (built in 1924) was designed to replicate the courtyard between two Egyptian temples at a time when the world was fascinated with the 1922 discovery of King Tut's tomb and Egyptian history. Beginning with the silent films (the premier was Zane Grey's *Wanderer of the Wasteland*) and supporting pipe organ music, it is now a venue for live theatre and screening Sundance films. It's just one of the places in this city that has always welcomed travelers.

SAN LUIS OBISPO

CALIFORNIA

The name San Luis Obispo de Tolosa is Spanish for "St. Louis, the Bishop of Toulouse." Originally founded as a mission by Spanish Franciscans in 1772, its name was to honor a 13th-century bishop, Louis of Toulouse, France. The mission and its surrounding area grew in population and is now considered one of the oldest communities in California.

To this day, the mission still stands in the center of downtown and in 1970, almost 200 years since its founding, the dedication of Mission Plaza was celebrated.

But celebrations in downtown San Luis Obispo are neither unusual nor infrequent.

If you plan to visit San Luis Obispo, try to be there on Thursday because in this downtown every Thursday night is Farmers Market. But this is not your usual farmers market. Six blocks in the middle of downtown are closed off where more than 120 vendors are located within a street party atmosphere. Entertainment acts are provided at each intersection. The crowds spill out over the sidewalks and soon the streets are filled with a wall-to-wall sea of slow-moving shoppers. The Farmers Market is an authentic celebration of community for citizens inside, and outside, the city limits. Parking spaces are packed for blocks and blocks in all directions. In the summer, crowds have been estimated as high as 10,000. It's an enjoyable blending of arts and agriculture, old and young, city and country, past and present—and it happens every Thursday!

Visitors to San Luis Obispo leave with an awareness of having experienced a unique evening they will not soon forget. The word continues to spread far beyond the local market area, and it's no surprise to those who have ever spent a Thursday in this friendly market festival to read that San Luis Obispo is "one of our country's friendliest towns."

The friendly, welcoming atmosphere of this community is a natural magnet for tourists who now represent a major component for the local, and regional, economy. The county shares the same name as the city and the motto of San Luis Obispo County is "Not for Ourselves Alone."

Driving along State Route 1, visitors find much to enjoy. The top agricultural crops are strawberries and grapes, and the ocean drive north soon leads to San Simeon and a National Historic Landmark, Hearst Castle.

The mansion and surrounding grounds are located on "La Cuesta Encentada" (The Enchanted Hill), overlooking the Pacific Ocean.

And Hearst Castle also has an ongoing connection to another American story, the emergence of American journalism. William Randolph Hearst's acquisition of *The San Francisco Examiner* in 1887 was the first step in building the nation's largest newspaper chain of more than two dozen newspapers in many of America's largest cities.

Hearst subsequently added magazines, radio and movie newsreels to his publishing empire and a fictionalized version of his life was made into a motion picture, *Citizen Kane*. The film, whose director, producer and star was Orson Wells, has often been listed as the best film of all time and was released on DVD in 2011 to celebrate its 70th anniversary.

Surrounded by the beauty of beaches, mountains and wineries, San Luis Obispo has been called the "happiest city in America." Local citizens say some of the reasons for that happiness are a ban on public smoking, the addition of bike valets, a vibrant town square, and wide sidewalks, the same ones welcoming thousands downtown every Thursday evening.

Reflecting on the wonderful weekly interaction of city and country, I am reminded of the following quotation:

> Yet it remains an unalterable truth that just as a sound mind depends on a sound body, so the health of cities depends on the health of the rural areas. . . . To restore a proper balance between city and rural life is perhaps the greatest task in front of modern man.
>
> —E.F. Schumacher
>
> *Small Is Beautiful: Economics As If People Mattered*

SANTA FE

NEW MEXICO

In Santa Fe, New Mexico (population 70,000), two buildings—one old and one new—stand in close proximity, and share a common mission.

One building, the New Mexico History Museum, located on the historic Santa Fe Plaza, opened in May 2009. The other building, the Palace of Governors, was originally constructed in 1609.

There is a 400-year difference in age, yet they stand together as symbols of the city in which they reside.

Santa Fe has long been a favorite destination for those fascinated by the history and culture of the American Southwest.

Although there are indications of Pueblo villages in the area as early as 1150, it was not until 1607 that a town was founded and given the name *La Villa Real de la Santa Fe de San Francisco de Asis*—the Royal Town of the Holy Faith of Saint Francis of Assisi. Three hundred years later, in 1912, New Mexico became the 47th state, with Santa Fe (meaning "Holy Faith") as its capital (population was approximately 5,000).

The residents of Santa Fe are aware that everything, even history, should be refreshed over time.

On the New Mexico History Museum website, the mission statement reads:

> The New Mexico History Museum . . . has evolved into a first-class museum project, spurred by the national rethinking of the role history museums play in communities. They are no longer attics or basements full of long-forgotten objects. They are now places that partner in education, civic engagement, and social change.

It is intended that the new museum will assist in doing what Santa Fe, through the years, has always done—"change the way that New Mexicans and visitors understand state history and the history of the nation."

It seems that everyone finds something about Santa Fe that leaves a lasting impression.

For some, it's the Santa Fe Opera, founded by John Crosby when he built a 480-seat wooden theater and opened July 3, 1957, with *Madame Butterfly.* Today, the 2,200-seat amphitheater is surrounded by a beautiful New Mexico setting and is not only one of the oldest opera festivals in the U.S., but one of the very best. The total summer audience exceeds 85,000, with at least half coming from outside New Mexico (including 25-30 nations).

Crosby, who served as general director for 44 seasons, "made opera bloom in the desert," according to *Los Angeles Times* music critic Mark Swed. "With Santa Fe Opera, you could say that festival opera came into its own in America."

For others, it's the Georgia O'Keeffe Museum, the world's only museum dedicated to an internationally known American woman artist. Known to many for her large-scale depictions of flowers, O'Keeffe, one of many artists and writers who have been attracted to the area, moved to New Mexico in 1949, after continual visits during the previous 20 years. Her two homes, about an hour's drive north of Santa Fe, in Abiquiu and Ghost Ranch, are under the care of the museum, which is within easy walking distance of the Plaza.

And there's the Santa Fe Plaza, itself a National Historic Landmark and truly "the heart of Santa Fe." The place where Spanish, Native American and Mexican cultures come together in daily celebration of past and present by 100,000 annual visitors. For almost 100 years, the Santa Fe Indian Market has been centered on the Plaza as 900 of the best Native American artists display their work at the largest Native American art show in the world.

On the Plaza stands the La Fonda hotel, which "occupies the oldest hotel corner in the United States, in the oldest U.S. capital city, and dates back some 400 years," writes Lyn Bleiler, "offering a mix of Santa Fe's art and cultural history with luxurious modern comforts . . . often referred to as a living museum." When Simone de Beauvoir visited Santa Fe in 1948 she wrote "La Fonda is the most beautiful hotel in America. Perhaps the most beautiful I have ever seen in my life."

Not far from the Plaza is the Loretto chapel, another popular stop for the hundreds of visitors. Many come because they've heard of the mysteries of the unusual helix-shaped staircase. Built in the 1870s, the legend attached to its construction left no information regarding the identity of the builder nor the way it could be built with two 360-degree turns yet no visible means of support.

When *Travel + Leisure* magazine conducts its periodic survey of the "U.S. Best Cities" it's no longer surprising to find Santa Fe high on the list, even in the top five. With no regard for size, the survey is based on consideration of such things as landmarks, historic sites, culture, food, friendliness, shopping and overall value. Some say they don't know of any other city like Santa Fe, that's probably why the locals like to call it "The City Different."

Or, as D.H. Lawrence wrote in the early 1900s, "Touch the country [of New Mexico] and you will never be the same again."

TAOS

NEW MEXICO

When arriving at Taos Pueblo, a visitor will be greeted by a sign containing the following message:

The Red Willow People of Taos Pueblo welcome visitors as they have for over 1,000 years. To visit the living village is to walk into a sacred place where life continues from the earliest of human existence. Little has changed here in the high desert village. From the people to the pristine landscape, Taos Pueblo continues to enchant visitors old and new.

It is said that when the first Spanish explorers arrived in this area of northern New Mexico they thought they might have found one of the golden cities of Cibola (a notion encouraged by the glittering light that emanated from mica, a mineral in the clay soil used to build the pueblo).

Taos Pueblo, the oldest continuously inhabited community in the U.S., reaches five stories in height at some places, and some 150 residents continue to live there without running water or electricity. Truly, "little has changed here."

In 1992, Taos Pueblo received the UNESCO designation of a World Heritage Site, joining a list with India's Taj Mahal and the Great Pyramids of Giza.

Several shops in Taos Pueblo are operated by third-generation family members who are continuing a heritage of handmade arts and crafts, including painting and pottery making. And the arts continue to be a major factor in the life not only of Taos Pueblo, but of the entire town.

There is, and has always been, a deep appreciation for the natural artistic beauty of this area. Joseph H. Sharp is considered "the artist who started it all" after a visit in 1893. The word spread among artists in America and Europe, particularly Bert Phillips, Ernest Blumenschein, E.I. Course, Oscar Berninghaus and Herbert Dunton. This group became the founders of the Taos Society of Artists, holding their first meeting on July 1, 1915, with the singular purpose to promote showing and selling of art. The group added other members and eventually disbanded in 1927. But their efforts and the continuing appreciation of artists for the enchanting atmosphere, the big, blue sky, the huge clouds and the stunning sunsets has resulted in Taos becoming an international art market, claiming more artists per capita than any other place in the world.

The homes of several of the early artists are now museums, some listed in the National Registry of Historic Homes. One example is the Blumenschein Museum in the Historic District of Taos.

Another is the Fechin House that preserves the story of Nicolai Fechin, who fled the Russian Resolution, arriving in Taos in 1927, bringing with him his family and his art. His house is now home of the Taos Art Museum, a result of community-minded citizens, perhaps with much the same spirit as their predecessors in the Taos Society of Artists, who formed the Board of Taos Art Museum, restored and renovated the Fechin house and in 2003 added another chapter to the Taos story.

In many ways, the story of Taos is a story of art (there are more than 80 art galleries and museums in Taos).

It must be said, however, that the story of Taos is not a story of the artists alone. It also is the story of protectors and preservationists.

The outside adobe surfaces of the Pueblo walls are continuously maintained by replastering with thick layers of mud and the inside surfaces are given thin washes of white earth to preserve the spirit of the place.

In the recognition of the Taos Pueblo as a World Heritage Site, there is this statement:

> Protection of this living cultural heritage takes vigilance
> and the continuing work of a committed community.

WINSLOW

ARIZONA

Sometimes all that is necessary to make a strong case for visiting a town is one good story about one distinctive building. An example is La Posada in Winslow, Arizona, a grand example of a destination hotel.

Some know Winslow because of the 1972 Eagles/Jackson Brown song "Take it Easy." At the mention of Winslow, they immediately break into the familiar lyrics, especially the line "Standing on the corner in Winslow, Arizona." And it seems there are almost always people there, standing on that corner, "with the girl in a flatbed Ford slowin' down to take a look. . . ." painted on the corner building to complete the photo-op.

A few historians of aviation history might even remember that in 1929 Charles Lindbergh, then the head of the Transcontinental Transport technical committee, selected Winslow as one of 12 critical refueling stops on the first American transcontinental passenger line.

And now, the La Posada is giving increasing numbers of drivers a new reason to make Winslow a critical refueling and overnight stop across the western U.S.

The story begins in 1930 when Fred Harvey decided to build a major Harvey House railroad hotel at the Santa Fe Railroad headquarters in Winslow. He selected Mary Elizabeth Jane Colter to design the hotel, which she considered her masterpiece. La Posada opened May 15, 1930, the year after the economic crash of 1929. It closed 27 years later, in 1957, and remained closed for some 40 years. Demolition was considered.

In the late 1990s, a plan to restore La Posada gained momentum. Today the La Posada provides an opportunity to personally experience the best of the railroad passenger era. In fact, a visitor may arrive and depart by Amtrak passenger train each day, only a few steps away from the hotel. Shopping, dining, an art gallery and a music room are available, as well as a large garden, without leaving the hotel grounds.

"Now, Colter's beautifully designed interior has re-emerged," wrote Susan Morgan in the *New York Times* (Feb. 9, 2007): "arched doorways, hand-painted glass windows, glittering tin chandeliers, Southwestern hand-built furniture and whimsical jackrabbit ashtrays."

REGARDING PARIS

A CLOSING COMMENT

Early in the 21st century, when the editors of *Lonely Planet* conducted a survey asking travelers to nominate their favorite cities, the top five "held no major surprises"—Paris, New York, Sydney, Barcelona and London.

They went on to write, "It was interesting to see just how the city standard is set by Paris. There are several other cities in this book that claim the reputation by association: Budapest, as the Paris of Eastern Europe; Beirut, as the Paris of the Middle East; Buenos Aires, as the Paris of the South; and Melbourne, as the Paris of the southern hemisphere!"

What is it that confers upon Paris such a singular significance?

Over the years, several have attempted to explain its distinctivity with words, some even in song. Following are a few insightful comments.

> What an immense impression Paris made upon me. It is the most extraordinary place in the world.—Charles Dickens

Paris is the only city where you can step out of a railway station—and see, the Seine with its bridges and bookstalls, the Louvre, Notre Dame, the Tuileries Gardens, the Place de la Concorde, the beginning of the Champs Elysees—what other city offers as much as you leave a train?—Margaret Anderson

There is an atmosphere of spiritual effort here. No other city is quite like it. I wake early, often at 5 o'clock, and start writing at once.—James Joyce

You can't escape the past in Paris, and yet what's so wonderful about it is that the past and present intermingle so intangibly that it doesn't seem to burden.—Allen Ginsberg

The whole of Paris is a vast university of Art, Literature and Music. . . it is worth anyone's while to dally here for years. Paris is a seminar, a post-graduate course in Everything.—James Thurber

A walk about Paris will provide lessons in history, beauty, and in the point of life.—Thomas Jefferson

Taken together, Paris seems to be an appealing and skillful mixture of:

- distinctive sights (the visible)
- atmosphere of spiritual effort (the invisible)
- past and present deftly intermingled (balance)
- art, literature and music (illumination)
- history, beauty and the point of life (meaning)

Reading the above, I was reminded of an article in *Condé Nast Traveler* by Sir Harold Evans titled "I'll Always Have Paris." But the Paris in his story is Paris, Illinois, population 10,000. Reflecting on his visit, Evans wrote,

> In Paris, I felt I was very close to the old Midwest and the pioneers who had turned the wilderness into America's larder. . . . The primitive vigor remained, titanic and miraculous but accompanied, I thought, by those original qualities of devoutness, simplicity, patience, deep independence of thought and neighborliness.

In reflecting on the treasured places in this book, it seems there is something of Paris in each of them. Hopefully, each of us has our own "Paris" that can "claim the reputation by association." It is our treasured place.

...................⌒✦...................

There are 53 places in the world named Paris
and 22 of them are in the United States.

NOTES

Many of the sources of information have been cited in the appropriate places within the pages of this book. On the following pages we have included, in some cases, additional information related to those sources and, in other cases, material that might be of interest to those who would like to read further regarding a particular place or person.

Annapolis, Maryland
- Jane W. McWilliams, *Annapolis, City on the Severn: A History*, Johns Hopkins University Press, 2011
- History of United States Naval Academy, **usna.edu**

Bar Harbor, Maine
- Town History, barharborhistorical.org
- Bill Trotter, "Bar Harbor Park Named Top 10 Public Space by National Organization" *Bangor Daily News,* October 9, 2012
- The Hudson River School, National Identity and America's National Parks, **nps.gov**
- John D. Rockefeller and the Carriage Roads, **visitmaine.com**
- Beckie Strum, "A Look at David Rockefeller's Real Estate Gifts," *Mansion Global,* March 20, 2017

Berkeley Springs
- Jeanne Mozier, The Early Days of Bath, **berkeleysprings.com**
- The Ice House is the center for the arts in Morgan County, **macicehouse.org**

Canton, Ohio
- Ohio History Central, **ohiohistorycentral.org**
- History of the Pro Football Hall of Fame, **profootballhof.com**

Cooperstown, New York
- Jim Lewis, "Yes, There Really is a Cooperstown," *Travel + Leisure*, January 2017
- Stephen Clark, "How It Came to Be in Cooperstown," June 10, 2014, **mlb.com**
- Thomas Boswell, *Why Time Begins on Opening Day*, Doubleday, 1984

Dearborn, Michigan
- A. James Rudin, "The Dark Legacy of Henry Ford's Anti-Semitism," Religion News Service, October 10, 2014
- Henry Ford Museum of American Innovation, **thehenryford.org**
- Brian Stone, "What If America Looked Like Dearborn, Michigan?" *Huffington Post*, February 26, 2016, **huffpost.com**

Gettysburg, Pennsylvania
- Information regarding the Gettysburg National Military Park Museum, the David Wills House, and the Eisenhower National Historic Site is available through the National Park Service, **nps .gov**
- Emma K. Young, "They Will Remember Gettysburg," A Brief History of the Rupp Family and the Rupp House and Tannery (Friends of the National Parks at Gettysburg, 2002)

Holland, Michigan
- Michael Corn, Margaret Aro and Christine Brozyna, "Low-Key Michigan Town One of the Happiest Places in America," ABC News, February 17, 2010, **abcnews.go.com**
- Tulip Time Schedule and Dutch Heritage, **tuliptime.com**
- Randy Vande Water, "Tulip Time Honored Lida Rogers On Silver Anniversary," *Holland Sentinel*, May 7, 2017

Hope, New Jersey
- Joyce Carol Oates, "Joyce Carol Oates Goes Home Again: The celebrated writer returns to the town of her birth ['the rural crossroads of Millers port, on the Tonawanda Creek, and the city of Lockport on the Erie Canal'] to revisit the places that haunt her memory and her extraordinary fiction," *Smithsonian*, March 2010

Lewes, Delaware
- St. Peters Church, **stpeterslewes.org**

Lexington, Concord, and Sudbury, Massachusetts
- The Wayside: Home of Authors, **nps.gov**

Mystic, Connecticut
- Charles W. Morgan: The Last Wooden Whaleship in the World, **mysticseaport.org**

Newport, Rhode Island
- Brief History of Newport, Newport Historical Society, **newporthistory.org**
- George Washington's letter, **tourosynagogue.org**

Peterborough, New Hampshire
- Bud Kliment, "The Birth and Life of an American Classic: 'Our Town,'" from the Pulitzer Files, **pulitzer.org**
- Brooks Atkinson on *Our Town* by Thornton Wilder—February 4, 1938—Henry Miller's Theater, *The New York Times Book of Broadway: On the Aisle for the Unforgettable Plays of the Last Century*, edited by Ben Brantley, Macmillan, 2001

Stockbridge, Massachusetts
- Norman Rockwell: A Brief Biography, Norman Rockwell Museum, **nrm.org**
- Chris Bury via GMA, "New England Town Stages Rockwell Painting," ABC News, December 13, 2009, **abcnews.go.com**

Asheville, North Carolina
- **romanticasheville.com** (See "Architecture")

Athens, Georgia
- Justin Hubbard, "1996 Olympic Games Put Athens, Sanford Stadium In Front of a Global Audience," *Athens Banner-Herald,* May 7, 2016
- A Brief History of Athens, **visitathensga.com**

Beaufort, South Carolina
- Annette Thompson, "Beaufort by the Water: Explore the Lowcountry Charms of This South Carolina Village," *Southern Living,* April 12, 2017

Charleston, South Carolina
- Richard Nalley, "The Best of Charleston," *Forbes*, April 17, 2009
- Kirk Brown, "Former Charleston Mayor's Museum Mission: 'I can't rest until I've done my duty,'" *Anderson Independent Mail*, March 8, 2018
- A Great Walking Tour of Charleston, **charlestonlowcountry.com** (See "Charleston Touring Itineraries")

Henning, Tennessee
- Personal interview with Alex Haley, April 30, 1987, West Texas Digital Archives, ACU Library, video

Hot Springs, Arkansas
- **hotspringsbaseballtrail.com**
- Hot Springs National Park, **nps.gov**

Key West, Florida
- **keywesttravelguide.com**

Oxford, Mississippi
- Newt Rayburn, "153 Years Ago, August 22, 1864: The Burning of Oxford, Mississippi," *The Local Voice,* August 22, 2014
- Faulkner's Obituary, *New York Times*, July 7, 1962
- Faulkner's Nobel Prize banquet speech, **nobelprize.org**

Rock Hill, South Carolina
- Lynn Willoughby, "The Good Town Does Well: Rock Hill, S.C., 1852-2002," Rock Hill Sesquicentennial Committee
- **riderockhill.com**

St. Augustine, Florida
- Hotel Ponce de Leon, St. Augustine, Florida, **historic-structures .com**
- Henry Morrison Flagler biography, **flaglermuseum.us**
- Castillo de San Marcos, **nps.gov**

Williamsburg, Virginia
- Colonial Williamsburg Foundation, Project Gutenberg Self-Publishing Press
- In Williamsburg, tourists are not just outsiders looking in, **travelchannel.com**

Columbus, Indiana
- Clay Risen, "By Design: Over the past half-century the small town of Columbus, Indiana, has turned itself into a showplace of modern architecture," *Smithsonian*, December 2005
- The Cummins Foundation, History and Mission

Durango, Colorado
- David Peterson, "Durango, Colorado: Small-Town Life in the West," *Mother Earth News*, September/October 1989
- List of World Heritage Sites, **whc.unesco.org**

Galena, Illinois
- Mark Yost, "Ulysses S. Grant in Galena," *Wall Street Journal*, April 27, 2011

Green Bay, Wisconsin
- Rick Reilly, "Be the 74,659[th] in Line!" *Sports Illustrated*, October 15, 2007
- Travis Pipes, "Lambeau and his Legacy: Lombardi's Equal," *Lombardi Ave*, June 11, 2013
- James Kouzes and Barry Posner, "Mental toughness is . . . ." as quoted in *The Leadership Challenge*, p. 271, Jossey-Bass, 1987

Greenfield, Indiana
- Riley quote on persistence, *The Consolidated Encyclopedic Library*, edited by Orison Swett Marden, vol. 17, p. 5004, 1903

Independence, Missouri
- Truman: HST Biography—Truman Library, **trumanlibrary.org**
- Harry Truman and Independence, Missouri, **nps.gov**

Iowa City, Iowa
- Literary Walk, **iowacityofliterature.org**

Paducah, Kentucky
- Columbia Theatre, **palmerwestport.com**
- **johncashon.wordpress.com**, "How Paducah, Kentucky, Got Its Name"

Sturgis, South Dakota
- Things To Do in Sturgis, **yahoo.com/news**
- Things to Know to Survive Sturgis, South Dakota, Bike Week, **travelingmom.com**

Creating a Sense of Place
- Luke Barr, "At Home in Provence," *Travel + Leisure*, April 2009
- Maureen B. Fant, "Small is Beautiful; Orvieto, Italy, *New York Times Magazine*, May 9, 1999
- Joel Kotkin, "There's No Place Like Home, Americans are Returning to Localism," *Newsweek*, October 10, 2009

Ashland, Oregon
- Oregon Shakespeare Festival, **osfashland.org** (See Our History and Ashland and the Festival)

Astoria, Oregon
- Jane Jacobs, *The Death and Life of Great American Cities*, Random House, New York, 1961

Billings, Montana
- John Steinbeck, *Travels with Charley: In Search of America*, Viking Press, 1962

Boulder City, Nevada
- The Historic District of Boulder City, Nevada (brochure), **bcnv.org**

Carmel-by-the-Sea, California
- Mark Frost, *The Match: The Day the Game of Golf Changed Forever*, Hyperion, 2007
- Eric Levin, "Promising a New Spirit—and Freedom of Ice Cream—Clint Eastwood Tackles His Toughest Role: Mayoral Candidate," *People*, March 17, 1986

Cheyenne, Wyoming
- Frontier Days Volunteers, **cfdrodeo.com**

Cody, Wyoming
- James Michener, *The Quality of Life*, Girard Bank, 1970

Grand Canyon Village, Arizona
- Virginia L. Grattan, *Mary Colter—Builder Upon the Red Earth*, Northland Press, 1980

Ketchikan, Alaska
- Dave Kiffer, "Ketchikan Took Shape 120 Years Ago," **sitnews.us**
- Abigail Roberts, "Preserving Identity & Art: Totem Heritage Center," National Endowment for the Arts, August 20, 2013

San Luis Obispo, California
- Dan Buettner, "Thrive—Finding Happiness the Blue Zones Way," *National Geographic,* 2011

Santa Fe, New Mexico
- Allan Kazinn, "John Crosby, 76, Dies: Started Santa Fe Opera," *New York Times*, December 17, 2002
- Chris Pasles, "John Crosby, 76, Founder of the Santa Fe Opera Was Called a Pioneer for Innovative Repertory," *Los Angeles Times,* December 17, 2002
- Lyn Bleiler, "A Legend Going Strong," *New Mexico Magazine*, January 2012

Taos, New Mexico
- D.H. Lawrence, "New Mexico," an essay written in 1928, as referenced by Sharlene Goff, "New Mexico: Follow in the Footsteps of D.H. Lawrence," *The Independent,* January 6, 2002 (the D. H. Lawrence Ranch in the Taos area is open to the public)

Winslow, Arizona
- Susan Morgan, "In Arizona, A Railway Town Rediscovers a Touch of Past Glory," *New York Times,* February 9, 2007

INDEX